PLYMOUTH IN THE FORTIES AND FIFTIES

British Library Cataloguing in Publication Data

Chris Robinson
Plymouth in the Forties and Fifties

A catalogue record for this book is available from the British Library

ISBN 978-0-9569858-0-4

Written and illustrated by Chris Robinson
Design Ewan McKnight and Chris Robinson
© Chris Robinson 2011

First published 2011

Published by
Pen & Ink Publishing
34 New Street, Barbican
Plymouth PL1 2NA
Tel: 01752 705337/228120
Fax: 01752 770001
www.chrisrobinson.co.uk

Printed and bound in Great Britain by
Latimer Trend & Company Ltd
Estover Close
Plymouth PL6 7PL
Devon

CONTENTS

INTRODUCTION

Although titled 'Plymouth in the Forties and Fifties' this book essentially deals with the years 1945-1955: that intense and dramatic period of new building and reconstruction that saw the city centre rise from the ashes and the city boundary expand to encompass the new estates of Ernesettle, Ham, Honicknowle, Whitleigh and Efford.

Plymouth had been, per head of population and per acre, the worst bombed city in Britain (and for a full account of the early Forties look out for 'It Came To Our Door' written by Pat Twyford in 1945 with a revised version being published with the addition of over 400 photographs, by Pen & Ink in 2005). However although a decision was taken to clear most of the city centre and start afresh in order to realis the bold vision of the 1943 Abercrombie and Paton-Watson 'Plan for Plymouth', there were many familiar landmarks that had survived the ravaging fires started by enemy incendiaries. So it was that even this optimistic era of rebirth was tinged with sadness as one by one those often well-loved reminders of what Plymouth had been like before the war fell victim to the ball and chain of the developer. Meanwhile, away from the city centre itself, there were other losses that were even more keenly felt as many of Plymouth's oldest residences, shops and inns around Sutton Harbour were pulled down:

each demolition helping secure a license for a bright new building in some other part of the post-war landscape. It is a sad reflection on the drive to rehouse the displaced population that more Tudor and Jacobean buildings in the Barbican area were destroyed in the ten years after the war, than had been lost during the intermittent enemy bombing raids between 6 July 1940 and 30 April 1944.

In Devonport the situation was hardly any happier, as the Admiralty dithered and delayed their decision on just how much of the proud old town they wanted to requisition for their peace time programme. By the time they had drawn their lines and built their Dockyard extension walls, the community had come to realise that as a commercial shopping and entertainment centre it had been completely eclipsed by its old rival, Plymouth. At the same time, the third of the pre-1914 Three Towns, Stonehouse, was similarly left to wither on the vine.

Such is not to say, however, that the prevailing mood across the city was a gloomy one, far from it, as a spirit of optimism drove the Local Authority and the local population. Plymouth's rise from the ashes was to be more spectacular than that of any other city in the country and other authorities marvelled at the speed and at the extent of the redevelopment.

Opposite page: Plymouth, looking east c1945

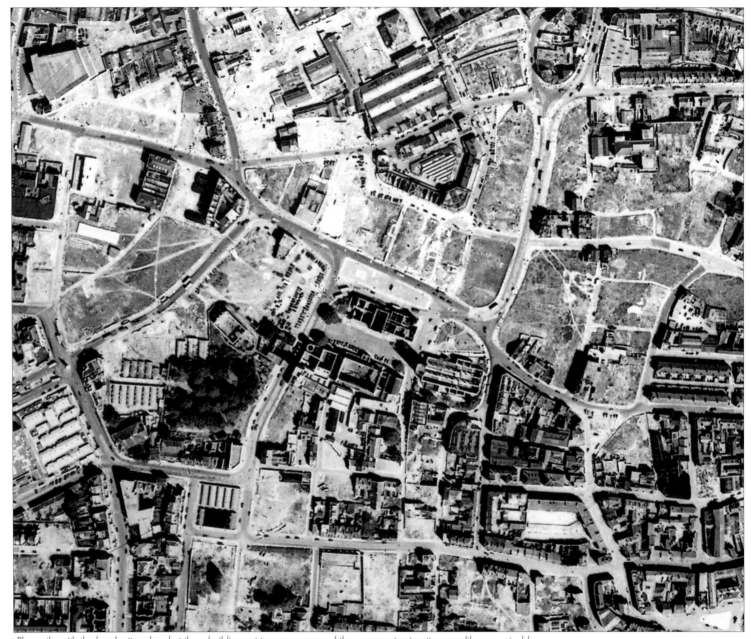

Plymouth, with the bomb sites clear but the rebuilding yet to commence and the pre-war street pattern readily recognisable.

With housing the main priority, it was a proud Labour Council that could claim, by the middle of 1949, that some 18,900 persons (almost 6,000 families) had been housed in new properties. The following year the first new City Centre store - Woolworths - had started trading, and then when Dingles opened on 1 September 1951 it was hailed nationally as the first post-war Department Store to be built in Britain.

With money and materials - and hence building licenses - severely restricted, Plymouth's fine new row of Portland stone shops and business premises lining the principal new axes of the centre - Royal Parade and Armada Way - made a pretty picture and people came from all over the West Country to marvel at the sight, and to shop in these state-of-the-art premises.

For a while picture postcard sales of photographs depicting shiny red buses driving up and down the great wide thoroughfare that is Royal Parade, alongside these splendid new buildings (all of them designed by nationally, and internationally, recognised architectural practices of the day) outsold the iconic images of the Hoe and the Sound and any other surrounding - and more obvious - attractions.

Socially too the mood was upbeat. There was still rationing, but the war was over. People made do: the women knitted and darned and dyed; the men worked, smoked, and drank in their local while the children played in the streets, scrambled around the bomb sites and made dens out of rubble and ruins.

Most people went to cinema regularly, a third went once a week, few people could afford their own car, most holidayed at home or went by train to the seaside, but maybe just for the day. Sporting events were well attended - football, speedway, greyhound racing, rugby. Amateur dramatic companies were well supported - the Tamaritans, Carmenians, Western College Players and many more besides. Most people listened to the radio (the BBC Light Programme or the Home Service) or made their own in home entertainment (television didn't arrive down here until the mid-Fifties). Few private houses had a telephone, many didn't even have an inside toilet and around a quarter of the population still didn't even have electricity.

Gradually however the years of austerity gave way to a more comfortable, more affluent era and during that process a new stage of the life-cycle started to find a voice of its own - the teenager.

The Education Act of 1944 had helped enormously by delaying the entry into the employment market for so many, as had the imposition of national service and the increasing provision of further education opportunities.

The increased spending power of this new section of society saw many dramatic shifts in our cultural fare, not least of which were the changes in the marketing of our popular music, as the bobby-socks era saw charts based on record sales take the place of charts based on sheet music.

Before long the influence of the teenager saw the average age of the truly popular stars fall, and fall again, until the young people were able to effectively demand their own generation of entertainers and with a sound that was anathema to parents and teachers alike - rock and roll.

So what was life like throughout that post-war, pre-rock'n'roll era? Flick through the pages of this book and you will see at a glance: streets with little or no street markings, and not that many cars; the last tram and the last of the horse-drawn roundsmen; Nissen huts and pre-fabs; coach parties and carnivals; factories and funfairs; servicemen and cigarettes; girls with hula hoops and skipping ropes; boys on cycle speedway bikes with home-made tabbards and football teams with ill-matching socks and shorts.

It's all here in black and white, recorded at a time when colour photography was the preserve of the professional and maybe one or two affluent individuals. For those who lived through it I hope you enjoy the trip down memory lane, for the rest I hope it gives you a flavour of the world your parents, grandparents or even great grandparents inhabited.

Above all, I hope that the endeavours of all those who worked hard to build a new City Centre that Plymothians would forever be proud of and which would stand out as an achievement unparalleled anywhere else in Britain, will forever be respected, and that subsequent generations will think long and hard before attempting to compromise the achievements of their forebears.

Chris Robinson *October 2011*

September 1945, one of Plymouth's last trams sets off from the bottom of Old Town Street.

THE DUST SETTLES

Although it was doubtless not intended to be a defining moment, it was, nevertheless, no real coincidence that within a couple of weeks of the final surrender of Japan, marking the conclusion of the Second World War, on 12 September 1945, the last tram service in Plymouth terminated.

Six years earlier, when the ultimatum for the German withdrawal from Poland passed unheeded and the British Prime Minister, Neville Chamberlain, had, with a heavy heart, announced that, as a consequence, 'this country is at war with Germany', there had been 27 tram cars in stock and available for duty. Now, however, there were only four that were still serviceable: Nos 154, 167, 158 and 165.

At 5pm, the 165 started out on its last journey, from the makeshift terminal at the bottom of Old Town Street (the track between St Andrew's Cross and the old terminus by the original Theatre Royal had been rendered unusable by war damage the previous year) and then, half an hour later, No.158 set off on the same route, to Milehouse, via Drake Circus, Mutley Plain and Peverell.

The last route: rounding Drake Circus.

9

At that time the rebuilding of Plymouth City Centre had yet to begin and the old street pattern was still clearly discernible, despite the shopping centre itself being barely recognisable. Long-cherished landmarks had been swept away as the demolition men came in and removed one after another hollow-eyed burnt-out shells of buildings and a steady procession of lorries removed seemingly endless loads of rubble.

For years now the middle of town had been a dirty, dusty bomb site with stone-strewn shortcuts being carved out between streets where previously there had been buildings. As pedestrians picked their way across the uneven terrain, unfamiliar vistas opened up and many buildings, that had previously stood in the shadow of their pre-war neighbours, now stood in splendid isolation, albeit with a demolition order almost certainly hanging over them.

All in all, the 1943 'Plan for Plymouth' had identified some 72 acres of prime City Centre land for redevelopment and that meant that precious few of those wartime survivors were destined to escape the ball and chain of the crane gangs brought in to flatten the sites.

There was one very significant central site where it was thought that it might be possible to preserve something that would be forever recognisable as pre-war Plymouth and that was the Guildhall Square. Here, although all three buildings had been gutted (apart from St Andrew's Church tower), from the outside at least, it looked, at first glance, as if little had changed, but there was daylight on the other side of those walls and a major programme of reconstruction would be required to put things right.

In the event, decisions were made to rebuild both St Andrew's and the Guildhall, however the northern line of the Municipal Building apparently intruded a matter of inches into the proposed line of Royal Parade and so it came down. None of these decisions were made quickly though, and for sometime the future of those ruins around the Guildhall Square hung in abeyance, although St Andrew's was kept going, after a fashion, as a 'Garden Church'. Open to the elements, attendances at the church were bound to be weather dependent and the early months of 1947, which heralded the coldest winter since 1880/81, tested the hardiest of any congregation.

Above: Three shells c.1945 - Municipal Building, St Andrew's and Guildhall.
Right: St Andrew's in the snow, 1947.

The immediate post-war scene, looking west down Bedford Street, with George Street running to the left of the Prudential Building and Cornwall Street to the right, with Frankfort Street between.

PLYMOUTH. POST-WAR GEORGE STREET, '46/47

PLYMOUTH. "SPOONER'S CORNER", '46/47.

Some unusual post-war picture postcards of Plymouth: George Street top, Old Town Street bottom.

Curiously enough other parts of the immediate post-blitz City Centre were reminiscent of a graveyard, with flat open areas of land being punctuated not by tombstones but by solitary buildings, some more impressive than others but all of them somewhat morbid reminders of a previous life and almost all of them ultimately doomed.

While examining the 'mortality' of these City Centre survivors it is worth bearing in mind that most of them had been standing for little more than half a century, if that. The heart of old Plymouth, then as now, being down around Bretonside and the Barbican, the City Centre footprint being primarily a nineteenth-century development.

George Street, like Old Town Street, was much earlier, however most of it was rebuilt during Queen Victoria's lifetime.

George Street had been laid out in the 1770s as an upmarket housing development on the edge of town, and then as Plymouth expanded, so those houses, which no longer enjoyed rural views, were pulled down and the street instead became one of Plymouth's principal retailing thoroughfares.

Old Town Street, meanwhile, was one of the oldest streets in the town, however as pressure for space where the footfall was greatest, and where improvements in transport called for wider streets, so a major programme of 'improvement' work was carried out in the 1890s and many ancient inns, taverns and retail establishments were sacrificed in order that taller and more spacious premises could henceforth line the sides of the road.

The surviving Drake Circus complex at the top end was one clear, turn-of-the-century example of this, while the much-missed Spooner's Corner, at the bottom end of the street, was barely 30 years old when it was flattened by enemy action during the Blitz (it was the third time in 40 years that Spooner's Corner had been destroyed by fire: after major conflagrations in 1902 and again in 1910).

Bedford Street too, was another product of late-Victorian redevelopment, with the distinctive plum-red-brick Prudential building of 1900, standing on the site of the much earlier Globe Hotel. Punctuating the western end of Bedford Street this site marked the old western entrance to the town – Frankfort Gate.

Bedford Street was the principal banking street of the town and again most of the properties there at the outbreak of the Second World War were not exactly what you would call ancient.

Around Charles Church there were older properties that survived the war, but none of them matched the seventeenth-century structure itself. The Household of Faith School, overlooking the church in Vennel Street, dated from 1798 (it was pulled down in 1958, after serving, post-war, as a local authority Domestic Science school).

Another house of learning that lasted even longer was the Victorian Technical College, just opposite and down from the Central Library, which, like the Museum and Art Gallery above it, dates from the early part of the twentieth century. The Museum survived the war relatively unscathed, the Library however was gutted and destined to be rebuilt, while the old Tech was to become a victim of the 1960s redevelopment that was to see a major roundabout created just below the Library.

Immediately above and below the Library and Museum are more turn of the century survivors in a block that, to date, has managed to find itself on the periphery of all the City Centre restructuring; not so fortunate have been the buildings on the other side of the road, stretching down to Old Town Street and across into Cobourg Street and out towards North Road, although, once again, it would not be until the 1960s that the demolition men would move in.

Late forties, early fifties Plymouth scenes, clockwise from top left: Charles Church; the old Tech opposite the Library; Pound Street looking towards the burnt-out Library; Tavistock Road and the City Museum and Art Gallery.

1947 Royal Parade starts to take shape, but there are still a number of pre-war survivors standing.

THE PLAN BECOMES REAL

Work began on producing the 'Plan for Plymouth' very soon after the Blitz had visited mass destruction upon the City. Made available for public perusal in 1944, come the end of the war it was still just a 'Plan', accepted only in principal.

'Certain it is that the city could not itself bear the financial burden of fully implementing the "vision of the city beautiful" as painted in the planners' book. Much would have to depend upon the measure of financial aid forthcoming from the national exchequer, and in this connection there was strong feeling that generous treatment was merited.' So wrote HP Twyford just after the war had ended in 1945.

It was clear that there was an appetite to realise much of what was in the Plan, but how close to that vision could the City afford to get, how close did it want to get, and how quickly could it get there?

With a very long waiting list of tenants looking for somewhere to live, housing had to be the Council's No.1 priority and to that end Plymouth was soon out of the starting-blocks and ahead of its blitzed counterparts across the country, winning commendations from Whitehall along the way.

Plymouth was also first to take advantage of the provisions of the 1944 Planning Act which gained Royal Assent in November that year and enabled those places that had been bombed to take control of redevelopment.

However, with so many men and resources being tied up in the provision of accommodation on the new housing estates, it was obvious that construction work in the City Centre was not going to be an easy process. A situation aggravated by the thorny issues surrounding the compulsory purchase of the City Centre site by the Corporation.

In March 1946 a major public enquiry was held outlining the proposals of the Corporation to acquire 'Declaratory Area No.1', the vast expanse we regard as being the City Centre. The proposal was that the City would compulsorily purchase 178 acres of land in the centre at 1939 values.

Not everyone was happy with the proposals, the Chamber of Commerce providing the main opposition. The new proposals marked a major departure from the private business owner and landlord situation and required the Corporation to rapidly expand their relatively new Estates and Valuation Department. But the City now had considerable power under Town and Country Planning Legislation and so the various compulsory purchase orders were issued and confirmed.

However, the Chamber of Commerce appealed the decision to the High Court and it wasn't until the appeal was withdrawn – in February 1947 - that the massive programme of preparation work, laying new utility pipes, ducts and services was started.

Top: *Royal Parade marks the beginning of the new City Centre.*
Bottom: *Last day of George Street being open to traffic.*

The following month, March 1947, saw a discreet granite kerbstone, bearing the date '21-3-47' but actually unveiled on the morning of Monday 17 March, appear on the edge of the massive new roundabout planned for the bottom of Royal Parade.

'It was at this spot, at the top of the old Raleigh Street that the first stake was driven for the layout of the new city centre. That was the point at which work started,' wrote Twyford two years later, adding: 'I hope that one day there will be a better commemorative recording than just those obscure figures which to any stranger, or to future citizens, might mean anything or nothing.'

Royal Parade of course was the key, the first of the two principal axes around which the new centre was to be laid out. Wider, both in terms of its traffic lanes and pedestrian provision, than anything the City had seen before, this new road was to be the flagship for the new Plymouth. Running due east-west and carrying what had previously been one of the most congested sections of the main A38 trunk road, Royal Parade marked a substantial departure from the pre-war street pattern and heralded a development that, across the board, bore little or no relation to the earlier layout.

But it was a protracted affair: 'It was not easy, and no-one will ever know the volumes of work performed by certain of the Corporation departments like those of the Town Clerk, the City Engineer, the City Architect, the Treasury and the Estates and Valuation. The difficulties that they fought and overcame were amazing. Tardiness in the granting of ministerial approvals and sanctions, shortness of staffs, especially on the technical side, limitation in labour and material, innumerable little irritations and emergency problems - all these things were encountered. It was, at times, almost amazing that the will to accomplish did not break under them. Fortunately, the planners were imbued with Plymouth's fighting spirit. It was as if they always had before them the motto which hung in Devonport Dockyard offices and workshops during the war – "The difficult we can accomplish now; the impossible may take a little longer".' (Twyford)

The Town Clerk was Colin Campbell, and it was his legal brain that guided the Corporation through what Crispin Gill described as the 'maze of new legislation'.

James Paton-Watson, a softly spoken Scotsman, who together with Professor Patrick Abercrombie had been the principal architects of the Plan for Plymouth, was still in the driving-seat as City Engineer. He it was who had persuaded the railway authorities to build a tower block at one end of Armada Way and the Imperial War Graves Committee to allow the extension to the War Memorial to complement his Plan at the other end.

Looking down the new line of Royal Parade with George Street, running diagonally from the Royal Cinema (bottom right) still cutting across it.

The man filling the new post of Estates and Development Valuer, meanwhile, was Bristolian, WK Shepherd. Appointed in 1946, he built up a department from nothing and *'did more for Plymouth than has ever been credited to him'*. (Gill)

Meanwhile, back on the building site that was Royal Parade, on 29 October 1947 the point was reached whereby the King and Queen could be received to officially inaugurate the reconstruction of the City Centre.

Curiously enough, it had been just hours after an earlier visit of George VI and Queen Elizabeth, on 20 March 1941, that the destruction of Plymouth had begun in earnest, when the Luftwaffe had unleashed a major aerial assault on the City. There had been nearly 300 air-raid alerts before that, and dozens of incidents, but nothing on that scale. Now, some six and a half years later, the City had dealt with the pain, cleared up the mess and started to rebuild.

The Lord Mayor, W Harry Taylor, proudly received the celebrated couple, who were clearly impressed at the speed with which Plymouth was progressing and who were happy to confer 'Royal' status upon the new principal axis of the City.

A commemorative tablet and a replica of Drake's Drum were unveiled at the foot of the flagstaff at the junction of Royal Parade and Armada Way – the very point to which all distances, to and from the City, are measured. It was a significant moment in time at an equally significant location and even more than the kerbstone at Derry's Cross it marked the dawn of a new era for the City.

Left top, middle and bottom: *20 October 1947, King George VI and Queen Elizabeth confer 'Royal' status on the principal axis of the new City Centre.*
Above: *Commemorative tablet and replica of Drake's Drum unveiled by the couple.*

King George VI and Queen Elizabeth approach the flagstaff with the Lord Mayor W Harry Taylor.

While housing was still the main priority, everyone could now see the bigger picture that was starting to take shape. It was almost as if the edge of the jigsaw puzzle had been laid down according to the Plan and now it was a question of looking for the pieces with the Portland stone cladding to see how they fitted into the picture in that very same Plan.

Of course, the big difference was that the new picture was being fitted on top of the old one and although parts of the slate had been wiped clean there were still a lot bits and pieces in the way: the Prudential Building; like the Plymouth Co-operative Furniture Emporium that had only been opened in Courtenay Street some 15 years earlier, in November 1932; the old bank in Bedford Street; the Corn Exchange, parts of the old Market, Market Avenue and Russell Street and the old Regent Cinema, now restyled the Odeon. These were all on the soon-to-be-cleared part of the jigsaw frame, while around the edges, below the line of Royal Parade and above Cobourg Street, there started to appear a number of Nissen huts. Pressed into service in a variety of guises, most of them as retail outlets for displaced City Centre stores, these semi-circular temporary structures could be erected in a matter of hours and with a smooth, flat-topped, white façade designed to disguise the inconvenient shape, they soon filled up with businesses anxious to retain a foothold in the heart of the old commercial shopping centre.

Opposite page and this page right top and bottom: Royal Parade is now in use but still no sign of building work either side of the new road.
Above: Illustration from the 1943 Plan for Plymouth showing the junction of Royal Parade and what would become Armada Way.

AS WE ROSE BEFORE SO SHALL WE RISE AGAIN, AND THOSE THAT FOLLOW RISE STILL GREATER

A more permanent solution was, of course, just around the corner, or rather, just over the road, but while Plymouth was, in many respects, ahead of the game in a national context, the pace for local business leaders was painfully slow.

It wasn't until November 1949, a little over two years since the King and Queen had 'opened' Royal Parade, that the site was at last cleared for what would become the flagship of the new centre, Dingles. Established by Edward Dingle, in Bedford Street some 70 years earlier, and occupying a similar site to its pre-war incarnation, the new building was to stand on the corner of the two principal axes, Royal Parade and Armada Way and it was the first new store to be started in the City Centre.

A few days later, however, work also began on Woolworths. Founded in America by Frank Winfield Woolworth, in February 1879, and operating on the basis that nothing should cost over five cents, the rapidly expanding business crossed the Atlantic in 1909 - in this country the benchmark became sixpence — and within ten years Woolworths had opened branches in Plymouth (Old Town Street) and Devonport (Fore Street).

Top left: *Hoardings announce the new stores to come.*
Bottom left and right: *Work begins (in November 1949) on the new Dingles department store*

Work on both Dingles and Woolworth's progresses. The two projects started within days of each other in November 1949.

As the work on the two big new stores progressed, the line of the new street running parallel to Royal Parade became increasingly well defined – this was the 'New' George Street. It was perhaps an odd choice of name as it bore little or no relation to the old George Street which ran to the south and west of the impressive Prudential Building rather than to the north and west of it, as Frankfort Street had done. There could be no disputing the fact that George Street had been one of the more upmarket shopping streets of pre-war Plymouth, but then so too had Bedford Street and that name had now disappeared. It may have been more logical perhaps to have called it Cornwall Street rather than New George Street, for most of Cornwall Street lay on the path of the new thoroughfare, but no, Cornwall Street was the name saved for the next street across in the new grid layout.

Curiously enough, however, three of the major north-south routes in the new centre retained the names of their pre-war counterparts with Raleigh Street, Courtenay Street and Old Town Street all roughly occupying the same footprint as their predecessors. East-west, it was a different story though, although perhaps by the time names were being looked for – for what would become Mayflower Street – the proximity in time to the 350th Anniversary of the sailing of the Mayflower outweighed the notion that the old Morley Street name might be preserved.

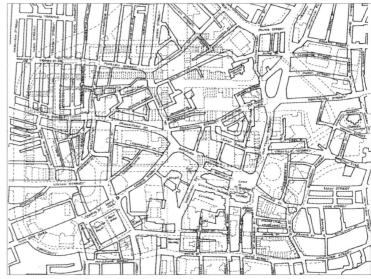

Left: *Two views showing work in progress on Dingles.* Above: *The new street plan starts to take over.*
Opposite page: *Late 1950, Woolworth's nears completion and the reroofing of St Andrews begins.*

Anxious to start trading from their new premises as soon as they possibly could, the management of FW Woolworth's opted to open in November 1950. It was exactly a year after work had begun on the new store and the building was still not properly finished. However, it meant that a little less than ten years after the worst of the bombing, Woollies had won the race to offer up a new shopping experience to Plymothians.

Great was the level of excitement, and great was the queue that waited patiently for the doors of the new store to open. With certain commodities still on rations, and the post-war period of austerity still not entirely over, people were used to queuing, but this was a fairly spectacular assembly as the almost exclusively female hoard lined back up from the doorway, along the fledgling New George Street and around into the remnants of Russell Street, right up to the Co-operative Wholesale store at the corner of Morley Street.

It's hard now to appreciate the impact made by the opening of this first part of the new shopping centre, but clearly it had more impact for most people than just the laying out of new road and pavements and the erection of street lights. Now at last there was something to see at eye level and above. In marked contrast to the tall, dark and rather gloomy late-Victorian buildings that had sprung up around the centre of Plymouth, this

Left: *Three pictures of the queue, that stretched around into Russell Street, for Woolworth's on opening day in November 1950. The scaffolding is still up, the building isn't yet finished, but it was ready to start trading on the ground floor.* Above: *The view from the south side of Royal Parade.*

new, light and low modern structure (it was even lower than its two 1930s neighbours, the Odeon [Regent] Cinema and the newspaper HQ, Leicester Harmsworth House) brought with it the promise of a bright new future.

The simple, unfussy lines were complemented by the broad, bright new street lights that cast a warmer glow over the streets below than any of their pre-war counterparts. The same spirit of optimism that had given the Labour Party a landslide victory after the war was still at large and as the country prepared for the much-vaunted Festival of Britain, on London's South Bank, in the summer of 1951, Dingles neared completion.

Opening the Festival, its Director, Sir Gerald Barry said the whole thing was a 'tonic to the nation', and if Plymouth itself thought that it was in need of a tonic, it certainly wasn't quite as badly off as some towns and cities around the country.

Indeed, when Dingles opened later that summer, on 1 September 1951, it was hailed as being the first large department store to have been built and opened in Britain since 1939.

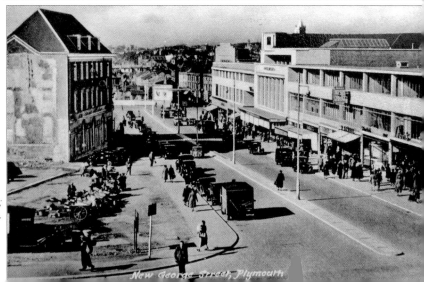

This page: The Woolworth building is finished and its neighbours to the east follow swiftly afterwards; meanwhile, the 1930 Odeon (formerly Regent) cinema and the 1938 newspaper offices look on.

As managing director, Mr JR Baker, and his second in command, Mr W Brimacombe, threw open the doors to the Royal Parade entrance that Saturday morning at 10 o'clock they were greeted by a warm cheer from the crowd that had been gathering since 6.30am.

Sheltered from the rain by the overhanging balcony (as it was described at the time) there was another throng waiting at the New George Street entrance for the doors of the 'up-to-date food hall' to open.

Estimates put the number that turned up to see the store on that opening day as around 40,000, the *Western Morning News* reporting that *'Nylons were the main object of the early arrivals'* and a queue very quickly formed at the Hosiery counter and at one point wound its way around several departments on the ground floor. Meanwhile, in the crowded ground-floor food hall at the New George Street end of the building, *'the grocery counters were besieged'*. Moreover, *'women who had secured the goods they required then stopped to admire a refrigerated window full of meat.'*

'It was an absolute mad house,' recalled one young girl who had been there on the day, *'it was virtually impossible to buy anything, there were so many people there.'*

Like Woolworth's, Dingles wasn't even completely finished when it first opened, furthermore, it wasn't even the second store to open after Woollies, as that honour went to the shoe shop alongside Dingles on the northern elevation – Dolcis.

Advertising from the outset as 'the most modern shoe store in Britain', Dolcis was, like Woolworths and Timothy Whites & Taylors (which also opened two weeks before Dingles), part of a national chain.

This page: *Dingles takes shape and is opened on 1 September 1951, just a week or two after its neighbours, Dolcis (shoes) and Timothy Whites and Taylors (chemists).*

Dingles was the first post-war department store to open anywhere in Britain, it was also the flagship of Plymouth's new city centre, note however that Drake Circus, the old market and the Corn Exchange are still standing, while the fate of the bombed-out Guildhall has still to be decided.

Old trees of Westwell Gardens survive on the southern side of Royal Parade, as do one or two old Westwell Street buildings, but the winds of change will soon blow down Armada Way.

All the more significant then, was the opening of Dingles, for not only was it the first construction in the reconstruction of Plymouth's shopping centre to be a local concern, it was also very much the flagship of that new centre.

'Built for and inspired by the people of Plymouth and the West Country' was the wording on the commemorative plaque that was unveiled on that first day of September, and as if to emphasise its very localness, there was a series of impressive murals painted by London-born artist Frederick Cook decorating the main stairwell: a Cornish fishing village (possibly Looe, near Polperro where Cook had his studio), a Dartmoor scene and another West Country landscape.

Of course Plymouth had long been the principal shopping centre for most of Devon and Cornwall: as the long-serving manager of Marks & Spencer, Raymond Hoskin was all too aware: he used to mark his Saturday takings with an H or A to the bemusement of head office, until he explained that H meant that Plymouth Argyle were playing at Home that Saturday and A meant that they were away. This was so that he could account, in his own mind why takings were that much higher on certain Saturdays, as men would come up from Cornwall for the day on the train and, as they headed off to the football, their wives would spend the afternoon in town, shopping!

As well as being the first 'total store' to open post-war, Dingles had another advantage over its competitors – it occupied the prime position in the proposed new shopping centre, at one corner of that bold new meeting point of Royal Parade and Armada Way.

Designed by Thomas Tait of Sir John Burnet, Tait and Partners, always with an eye on its strategic significance, the building made for a striking gateway to the new centre when approached from the Hoe side of Armada Way.

Tait would also act as a consultant to Alec French, who was responsible for the other crucial cornerstone of that entrance – the Pearl Assurance Building, a structure that, in terms of scale and basic design, very much mirrors the Dingles building.

With their respective towers part echoing that of the Guildhall on the other side of the road, together they formed part of a coherent streetscape that was a key element of Abercrombie's original vision.

With parking on its northern and western elevations and a large service court at the rear Dingles was then in a very good place and very well equipped for the second half of the twentieth century.

Two views of Dingles looking towards the Guildhall; note the bus stop by the corner of the store.

In addition to all the housing being erected around the city, work on the City Centre itself was now steaming ahead. In March 1951 with Woolworth's open and Dingles nearing completion, there suddenly appeared a whole colony of seemingly similar steel skeletons, each destined for a different and distinctive finish.

Ten years had now passed since the Blitz and all around there were signs of activity, providing the passer-by with something new to view every day.

When the Minister of Local Government and Planning, Hugh Dalton, visited Plymouth the following month he said he was *'delighted to see so many new buildings going up.*

'I went up to the roof of Dingles' building and had a very good view from there of the whole future developments that will take place.

'It will have been a blessing in disguise following the destruction of the last war that we have been able to re-plan the whole centre of Plymouth in this very much improved way as compared with pre-war days.

'In my view,' he added, *'the Plymouth City Council were very wise to complete their Plymouth Plan before the end of the war. They thus were able to get a flying start and there is no doubt that of the many other blitzed cities of the country, though some of them suffered damage as great as Plymouth, none has been quicker in getting forward with rebuildng.'*

However, the progress was far from plain sailing. Speaking at an event later that month, the Chairman of the Plymouth Reconstruction Committee, Sir Clifford Tozer, said that since the war's end licences had been issued in the city totalling over £2,000,000 and the majority of the buildings to which they referred should be completed within the next six to ten months. Tozer pointed out that there were currently 23 firms ready to start building as soon as their licences were granted, but to date only 11 had been. With the Government's decision on Plymouth share of the 1952 national building licence allocation about to be announced, Sir Clifford made the point that *'the longer the delay the greater the expense of eventual construction. Developers,'* he said, *'should be given the opportunity to start building before costs become prohibitive.'*

He said such a decision would also help to retain the large number of construction workers currently working in the city. Somewhat annoyingly, however, there was no quick reaction from Whitehall.

Top: *The Norwich Union building is erected on the old Spooner's Corner site.* Bottom: *One of Spooner's temporary post-war outposts further up Old Town Strreet and just down from the Bedford Vaults.*

With most workmen walking, cycling or bussing to work, the demand for city centre parking spaces was low. Note the fine view of the Royal Citadel on the Hoe, and the large building belonging to Pickford's Removal and Storage business on the north side of Whimple Street.

1951: the Norwich Union building nears completion and work is under way on the first phase of the new Plymouth Co-operative Society headquarters. Meanwhile, the blitz-surviving Prudential Building, at the end of what had been Bedford Street, has now almost all fallen to the ball and chain of the demolition men.

Norwich Union House is complete

Frustratingly, the Council's plans to extend Armada Way up to Citadel Road were also awaiting Government approval, as were the proposals to rebuild the Central Library. Meanwhile, Plymouth Sutton MP, Lucy Middleton, tabled a question in the House of Commons about the intended new General Post Office for Plymouth, as nothing had been heard about the scheme now for over two years.

With shortages of steel and of Portland stone, there were a whole variety of concerns behind what appeared to be the agonizingly slow progress. Addressing a Housing Conference in County Hall, London, in June 1951, Plymouth's City Engineer, James Paton-Watson told delegates that had the building licences been forthcoming the rebuilding of shops in the City Centre would be completed by now. But clearly it wasn't.

One delegate said that she was sorry to hear that the city was not using stone in its rebuilding scheme. The city, she said, had the chance to experiment in stone and it seemed a tragedy that the planners had not decided to set an example in this respect.

Paton-Watson replied that a facing of stone had been specified: admittedly this amounted to little more than a veneer of Portland stone. *'But,'* he pointed out, *'dressed stone is extremely expensive at 5s6d per cubic foot.'*

Amid laughter he added, *'If we should have any more bombing all the stone will be on the ground and we would be able to see through the buildings.'*

As it transpired, by the end of the year, another key element of the new City Centre was in place, as the Norwich Union Building on the corner of Old Town Street and Royal Parade was opened in October/November 1951.

Among the first to open in October was 'an old friend in the new Plymouth' H Samuel, who, with over 100 branches, claimed to be 'the Empire's largest jeweller'.

Local pharmacist Fernley Wallis, who'd been operating in the City Centre, at the old Market Gates, uninterrupted (apart from 28 days of dealing with bomb damage) since 1914 moved in on Thursday 15 November, on the same day as another local concern, the Plymouth Goldsmiths Co. who moved into No.5 & 7 New George Street, while for Woodhills' Plymouth Fashion House it was a return to the city centre after a ten-year blitz-induced absence. Among the other newly finished units were Kendall & Sons, specialists in all types of rainwear, Henry Dodgson, the ladies' coats and furs specialists, London Gown Co., HJ Modes, Leskin, Harwood, Swiss, Lockwood & Bradley and Hepworths.

The whole development - 16 shops and offices - was regarded as a triumph for the building contractors, who, in the first week of November 1951, took out an ad in the *Herald*: '*Ten months ago today, if you had looked at the site of Norwich Union House you would have seen nothing showing above ground level. Since that time this major building project has been carried to completion and is today officially opened. This really astonishing effort has been made and successfully concluded by Dudley Cole of Plymouth who desires to thank all those who by their loyal efforts and unremitting endeavour have made this feat possible.*'

With pride and pleasure we announce that

Hepworths are opening once again in Plymouth on Friday NOV. 23rd

The steelwork goes up for the new Marks & Spencer premises, top view looking across Tin Pan Alley to Central Methodist Hall, with Public Secondary in the distance.

Further up Old Town Street, Bovis were responsible for the new Marks & Spencer development which was ready for opening on 29 November.

Despite there being no special offers, some 2,000 queued up for the opening and quickly filled the partially completed store. Remarkably enough, work had only begun on the building in February, so even though the upper floors were not entirely ready, it was still quite an achievement.

Among the notable features of the new building were the staff-rooms, said to be among the most up-to-date in the country. The Air Force blue-and-maroon canteen, moreover, offered a three-course lunch for staff for just sevenpence h'apenny (3p) and a cup of tea for a halfpenny.

It was interesting too to note that the staff rest-room, replete with lemon-and-maroon leather and wicker chairs, bore a piece of stone from the pre-war store with the date 22 April 1941.

Two other stores opened that week: the well-known local music store, Moons, and the furnishing emporium of James Woodhouse & Sons, the latter being opened by the film actress Miss Mercy Haystead.

Left: *Almost ready.* Above: *29 November 1951, Marks & Spencer open with two policemen on hand to control the crowd!*

By now the roll-call of store openings was coming thick and fast. Another major chain, WH Smith's, had opened on Saturday 10 November at 10.30 am in No.16 New George Street.

Designed by WG Norris of Smith's own estates department, the building was erected by another local firm, Pearn Brothers. Replacing WH Smith's pre-war premises in George Street, the first floor (work on the second storey, with its library, fancy goods and toys was not expected to be completed until the New Year) was opened by the Lord Mayor, Alderman Randolph Baker, and every child there on that first day was given a free jigsaw puzzle.

Other firms up and running by the close of 1951 included Snell & Co, Salisbury's – the handbag people, Trueform, Barratts, Lawley's, and Willsons'. The latter, said to be the finest dress shop in the Willsons' chain, was opened by the 30-year-old film and radio actress Anne Crawford (who had come to prominence in 1943 with a handful of films, including 'Millions Like Us'. Sadly Anne was to make her last film in 1953 – she died of leukemia in 1956).

Designed on 'ultra-modern lines, incorporating American and Continental trends' Willsons' was finished in maroon and slate grey inside. The shop was notable for having 20 separate fitting-rooms.

Pearl Assurance Building marks the other side of the gateway to Armada Way, north of Royal Parade.

Woolworth's now with neighbours on either side.

All in all the best part of 30 new shops were open in time for Christmas 1951. Between them, it was said, they embraced virtually every household want, and it was hoped that another 30 would be opened in the coming year.

Most of these were firms whose licences were, eventually, granted in September 1951, just as the sands of time were running out and the withdrawal of some of that much-needed labour force looked likely.

Overall it was estimated that the number of men working on the reconstruction of the city centre had recently risen from around 700 to 800 and in the wake of those new licences, that number now looked set to rise to 900, with as many as 1,000 having been involved in the construction of Royal Parade, Old Town Street and New George Street.

Among the new developments kick-started before the year end we now had working sites for: the Trueform Boot Company, Boots the chemist, Harding & Sons, the local furnishing firm and Montague Burton's clothing store in Old Town Street (the latter embarked on a great, but ultimately unsuccessful, battle with the City Council to be able to have their trademark black exterior instead of Portland Stone).

Various views of another steel skeleton as Montague Burton's, on the corner of Old Town Street and Ebrington Street, rises out of the rubble – note Moons music store through the framework above.

An unusual glimpse of St Andrew's from the framework of the new Boots' building.

In New George Street work began on Manfield & Leon and FTB Lawson's, another long-established, locally run enterprise, while at the top end of Union Street, the new premises for the General Electric Company started to take shape, as did the new offices for the Royal Insurance Company at the top of Royal Parade and, the biggest of all this wave of development, worth about a quarter of a million pounds (roughly a third of this batch of building licences) – John Yeo's, which like Dingles, extended through from Royal Parade back into New George Street and which was also a locally run business.

Before the year was out it was announced that another of the great gaps in the Royal Parade frontage was to be filled as the Plymouth Reconstruction Committee passed plans for the four-storey Spooner's development.

Proposals for the seven-entranced Spooner building included a third-floor, a 300-seater theatre, with a 450-seater restaurant on the same level. Famous for the basement they had in the old Old Town Street store, there were plans to replicate that facility as part of what the proprietors proclaimed would be the largest building solely devoted to shopping in the city.

Mention of the theatre was interesting as just a few months earlier a licence application to rebuild the Grand Theatre in Union Street (with the largest stage west of Bristol) had been turned down.

The west side of Old Town Street near completion with the construction of Boots.

Meanwhile, in October, there was an announcement to say that Plymouth Guildhall was to be restored and further that a new concert hall was to be built at the rear of the Guildhall. Complete with large circulating foyers with cafés, bars and offices, the hall was to have seating for 2,000, with a sunken dance hall and exhibition space on the ground floor.

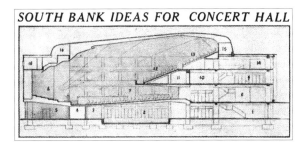

SOUTH BANK IDEAS FOR CONCERT HALL

Another gap in the Royal Parade frontage is filled in.

The new city centre takes shape, but note the number of terraces still to be sacrificed.

The following month, November 1951, speaking at a library lecture at the City Art Gallery, Dr ME Gordon of Plymouth City Council, outlined plans for a theatre capable of seating about 460 people as part of the reconstructed Athenaeum alongside the ABC Royal Cinema.

Generally speaking though, such rebuilding projects were happening at much slower pace than the commercial/retail reconstructions. St Andrew's Church was a good case in point: 'It is one thing for the War Damage Commission to agree to certain work being done and to agree to pay for it, but quite another matter to obtain a licence for the necessary materials and to carry out the work.

'We have to face the fact, that the powers that be look upon a church as non-productive. By that it is meant that they do not enrich the material life of the city with rates, taxes, and all the other benefits that come through commercial dealings.'

So ran a report in the *Church Review* monthly magazine of the parish of St Andrew's with St Catherine's Church.

However, the writer also noted that, *'though progress has been slow, work on St Andrew's [then reckoned to be about one-third done] has never stopped.'*

Crucially however, it rather looked as though work on some of the rising new commercial premises was about to stop as the Government announced a three-month ban on all new building work: the ban ran in tandem with the Government's new steel proposals.

In January the chairman and MD of John Yeo's, Mr WE Beckley, said that they needed about 590 tons of steel to complete their building, and the total allocation for the whole of Plymouth was just 405 tons over the next nine months. The situation was tense, as staggering the work inevitably made it much more expensive.

The situation was even worse for Spooners: their boss, John Bedford said his firm needed nearly 2,000 tons of steel.

For the first quarter of 1952 the Government decided to allow Plymouth just over 190 tons for those buildings already underway. It was far from enough, but considerably more than the allocations for Exeter (100 tons), Bristol (135 tons), Southampton (101 tons) and Portsmouth (85 tons).

Right: top and bottom; *The Pearl Assurance Building rises up on Royal Parade.*

A letter from the Minister of Housing and Local Government, Harold Macmillan, to the Town Clerk, Colin Campbell, spelt out the gloomy news. The immediate future looked bleak for Yeo's, Spooner's, Montague Burton's and the Ravensfelt Company (who were building five shops east of Dingles on Royal Parade).

At the end of January 1952 a group of eight Labour MPs led by Devonport MP, Michael Foot, tabled a motion condemning the proposed steel cuts as 'an unfair discrimination against areas still suffering from the results of enemy attacks'.

A couple of weeks later a deputation led by Michael Foot and Sutton MP, JJ Astor and including Sir Clifford Tozer, and Bert Medland (chairman and vice-chairman of the Reconstruction Committee), Colin Campbell and the city Estates and Development Valuer, WK Shepherd, presented their case to Ernest Marples, the Parliamentary Secretary to the Minister.

There was no immediate response; however, a week later Mr Marples was suggesting that licences would be more forthcoming and work would progress quicker if developers made more use of reinforced concrete rather than steel.

The use of steel, he argued, could be reduced by half or at least two-thirds, if reinforced concrete was used, and he suggested that the steel rods for this would be made available.

Left: *As the Pearl Assurance building starts to take shape so the boulevard that will become Armada Way is cleared of buildings.* Above: *Note the Nissen hut shops to the east of the Bank and Derry's Clock.*

This, according to City Engineer, Paton-Watson, would mean more walls and fewer windows: perhaps, he suggested, it was time to think of timber ... and brick too.

It all looked as though the 1943 vision was about to be somewhat compromised, but then news came that Plymouth could have a further allocation, 268 tons rather than 191, while Exeter and Bristol's allocation was reduced somewhat with smaller increases going to both Portsmouth and Southampton.

The deputation had not been without effect and a number of jobs, including the John Yeo project, was back on track.

There were yet other problems affecting the City Centre reconstruction. In April, the Ministry of Fuel and Power withdrew authorisation for the South Western Gas Board's new service centre on the corner of Union Street and Derry's Cross roundabout. The decision, however, did not affect the work that was already well under way on the adjoining General Electric Company premises, which were being rebuilt on their original site.

Answering a direct question from Sutton MP, JJ Astor, the assistant Post Master General said that he thought that work on a new Post Office, on the eastern rim of St Andrew's Cross Roundabout, was at least two years from being started.

Worse still, there had not been, in the six months after the end of October 1951, any new licences issued for new projects in the reconstruction area of the City and when in May 1952, Michael Foot asked when further licences might be granted, the Parliamentary Secretary to the Ministry of Housing and Local Government, Mr Marples, replied that it *'is not possible for the Minister to sponsor any new works in the reconstruction areas of blitzed cities.'*

It was not the news that local officials wanted to hear, and there were fears that the city centre labour force would drop well below its peak of nearly 1,000 to something in the order of 200, a figure that would make it even more difficult in the short term to realise future works.

Notwithstanding the various issues affecting overall progress, however, work did carry on – in pockets – and by the summer of 1952 the front elevation of Royal Parade, to the west of Armada Way at least, was starting to provide some sort of indication as to how impressive that principal axis of the new centre would look in the, hopefully, not too distant future.

Pearl Assurance Building top, *in skeletal form and below, almost ready to open.*

The new shopping centre takes shape but there are still a number of anomalies: like the buildings in the middle of Derry's Cross roundabout, the old Market buildings, properties in George Street and the Odeon Cinema in what was now New George Street. There was also still the barely 20-year-old Co-operative furniture emporium off Raleigh Street.

As the summer of 1952 arrived, mens' outfitters, Hope Brothers, announced their opening at 8 Royal Parade, on Saturday 19 July. That same month ladies' clothing chain Etam opened at No.13, as well as shoe specialists Stead & Simpson and London Tailors, Hector Powe.

Meanwhile, around the corner, later that same month Scotch Wools & Hosiery Stores, Moss Bros, the Singer Sewing Centre, Barnett-Hutton, and Freeman, Hardy & Willis – 'the largest shoe retailers in the Kingdom', who had temporarily been operating out of Glanville Street – started trading from units in the newly opened Pearl Assurance House building.

September saw another batch of new kids on the block as FST, Fit & Style Tailors arrived in Royal Parade, along with Sodens Furs. Relocating from temporary accommodation in Regent Street, Sodens made a splash with their Great Opening Fur Sale – offering a range of coats at half price from Kolinsky Coney at 10 guineas, Moleskin at 25, Beaver or Lamb at 29, Mink Marmot at 42 and top of the range Natural Musquash for 89 guineas, reduced from a whopping 178 guineas. All this at a time that the average housewife was said to spend between ten shillings (50p) and £2 a week on shopping.

In some respects the new arrivals, or rather the newly returning stores, seemed to be following each other in quick succession, but it could have been so much quicker and the lack of licences meant that by July 1952 there were some 70 skilled building operatives on the unemployed register at the Plymouth Employment Exchange, together with a number of experienced building labourers and 64 general labourers who, according to Mr ES Blackmore, the Exchange Secretary, 'would have been engaged on reconstruction a year ago'.

Top: 190 & 191 Union Street look increasingly incongruous in the middle of Derry's Cross Roundabout. Bottom: Meanwhile, the pre-war cinema (Regent now Odeon) sits out of line, but otherwise quite comfortably.

The awnings on Ebrington Street, Drake Circus and Market Avenue stand out on this sunny day, as much of the pre-war pattern is still in place more than a decade after the Blitz.

As the end of September loomed and still no new licences were forthcoming, the City was blessed with a visit from the Minister of Housing and Local Government, Harold Macmillan.

'I am here to learn and to listen', he said when quizzed about future licences, and refused to commit himself on the subject, or indeed the matter of the Guildhall, and its potential restoration.

'The Government will make a statement, probably when Parliament resumes.' Mr Macmillan added that his department was only concerned with the total amount of money to be allocated. It is up to the Corporation to decide whether it wants to build offices, shops, and the like, serving the commercial needs of the community, or municipal buildings such as halls and libraries.

The news was not well received by Michael Foot, or by former Plymouth Drake MP and member of Plymouth's Reconstruction Committee, Bert Medland.

Mr Medland pointed out that in each of the years, 1949, 1950 and 1951 the Labour Government had sponsored licences worth between £583,000 and £772,000, while so far, in 1952, the new Conservative Government had provided just £80,000.

In his defence the Minister pointed out that Plymouth had had 50 per cent of the allocation for the whole country, a fact that wasn't disputed, but clarified by stating that Plymouth had been ready for redevelopment while other places had not.

What is more, Plymouth was *still* ready with a further £1.25 million worth of building contracts on the table, including the Prudential, Spooners, Goodbodys, Lyons, Halfords, Olivers, Montague Burtons and the second phase of Marks & Spencer.

The latter were just one of a handful of firms who were spreading their redevelopment across a number of stages. Another was the Plymouth Co-operative.

As one of the largest retailers in town before the war it was clearly frustrating for the Co-op not to have their new premises open by now, but at least they had had the advantage of having one of the few surviving pre-war retail outlets in the City Centre.

In the event phase one of the new development was ready enough to part open by November 1952.

A large crowd arrived to witness the event and to explore the ground, and lower ground floors. Generally people were heartily impressed with the size and scale of the new store, marvelling at the

The doomed Co-op furniture emporium, barely 20 years old, stands alongside the building that will partially replace it. Bottom: Co-op president AN Stroud opens the first phase of the new Central Premises, with CR Westlake, Mrs Short, Mrs Moses and Mr Davey.

From the bottom right we see King Street running right up to the cinema where the old meets the new in Frankfort Street; note the pre-war Car Sales building below the two isolated Union Street shops, one of the few properties of that period destined to survive into the twenty-first century.

range of merchandise and the fixtures and fittings. The drapery department staff looked splendid in their wine-coloured dresses and attracted a great deal of attention.

Four weeks later, and just in time for Christmas, the first floor was opened up for the sales of millinery, fashions, carpets and lino, and four days after that – 8 December – the new tobacconist, on the corner of Royal Parade and Courtenay Street, was open for business.

The travel service office swiftly followed on the ground floor, moving from it's temporary accommodation in the former air-raid shelter facing Raleigh Street, while on the mezzanine floor (between the first and second floor) was soon to be found the new women's hairdressing department. Formerly fronting on to Frankfort Street in premises that only opened shortly before the war, the hairdressing salon had been housed briefly in Cambridge Street in the meantime, in premises that were now scheduled to come down to make way for further new developments.

A shampoo and set was then priced at 3/6d (17p) while a full perm could set you back anything between 15/- and 42/- (75p - £2.10). The average Co-op member spend per week with the Society at that time, incidentally, was just over one pound - which, if spent on food alone, represented the lion's share of a housewife's weekly spend.

Of course this was still only the first phase of the Co-op's new building, the second phase, roughly twice the size of the first, although already on the table, was awaiting a licence.

Once that licence had been obtained the plan was to hand over the existing, pre-war furnishing emporium to the Plymouth Corporation so that they could then demolish it and pay over compensation to the Co-op.

As it transpired that licence took some time to come through and it wasn't until late in 1954 that there was much to see in the way of building work on the corner of New George Street and Raleigh Street.

By the middle of May 1955 the ground floor of the second phase had been pressed into service, the pharmacy, optical and tailoring sections moving out of the old Emporium, which was now divided in half so that the western section of the building

Above: The new line of Buckwell Street and Breton Side appears.
Bottom: The eastern end of King Street, from the Co-op building site.

could be demolished. Meanwhile those departments that had been operating in temporary premises on the eastern side of Courtenay Street - footwear, grocery and confectionery - were now moved into the remaining eastern part of the old Emporium, which the Co-op, having sold it to the Corporation, now leased back.

It was all a bit frustrating and somewhat convoluted, but by May of the following year, 1956, the old Emporium had gone altogether and an impressive forest of steel had been erected from phase one in Royal Parade, around Derry's Roundabout and along Raleigh Street, to link up with the other corner site.

Throughout 1957 the building work continued and the Co-op's impressive new replacement for their pre-war Central Premises started to look something like a finished article. At this stage there was still no name for the Plymouth Society's new Headquarters - Central Premises had been ruled out, but there was no clear alternative.

It wasn't until 1958 that a decision was taken and members were informed that this retail and administration base was henceforth to be known as Co-operative House. Members were also told that the expanding Society had just acquired the interests of the Dartmouth Co-operative Society, which meant that most of the South Hams and South West Devon as far north as Tavistock, now fell within the Plymouth Society's sphere of influence as well as Launceston, Callington, Torpoint, Millbrook and Cawsand.

Top: *October 1956.* Bottom: *July 1957. Co-operative House built under direction of CWS architect WJ Reed, with the longest display window in the city - 22'6" by 7'6" and weighing 8 cwt.* Opposite page: *Work is ongoing on the Co-op and the Trustees Savings Bank, while Radiant House, at the bottom of the picture, is almost completed.*

Meanwhile, as work on the main Co-operative block had been inching along, work elsewhere in the City Centre had been gradually progressing too.

Just as November 1952 had seen the first phase of the Co-op building completed so too, another local concern, FTB Lawson opened in New George Street. With ironmongery, cutlery and tools on the ground floor and toys, hobbies and models spread across the first floor.

A few weeks before that, the new Charles Butler shop had started trading around the corner in Armada Way and in January 1953 they were joined by another fur coat specialist, Richfurs, in the Royal Parade corner unit of the Pearl Assurance Building.

Compared to other bombed cities around Britain, Plymouth was doing comparatively well, but it could have been (so much) better. When asked by Michael Foot in the

Opening-day advertisements from the local press.

House of Commons about the allocations for reconstruction work in 1953, Ernest Marples announced that Plymouth's share was £400,000 - the same as Portsmouth, Hull and Coventry - and £50,000 more than was being allocated to Bristol, Sheffield and Southampton and £100,000 more than Liverpool, Swansea and Exeter. While the likes of Birmingham, Manchester, Norwich, South Shields, Canterbury, Dover, Lowestoft and Great Yarmouth were much lower again.

However, there were those in Plymouth who felt that the city's provision was not enough … and there were those outside who felt it was too much and that Plymouth should now take a back seat.

But Michael Foot was certainly not one of them: *'Plymouth has had a raw deal this year and it would be a shocking thing if the city was now penalised for its enterprise in the years immediately after the war.*

'If the steel is there, as the Minister says it is, and if building labour is available, as there is in Plymouth, then it would be quite wrong to favour the authorities who have been lagging behind.'

In the event the pressure exerted by the Plymouth MPs and the Corporation paid off and Plymouth again fared rather better than other authorities and was allocated a further £600,000 bringing the total for the year to over £1 million (although over £200,000 of that was for work already in hand, rather than new works).

Among the new developments that could now be started were the new Prudential Building, the second stage of the Royal Assurance Building. Halford's (cycles), Oliver's (shoes) and another Timothy Whites & Taylors. The green light was also given to a number of projects beyond the city centre: Brown Brothers in Stonehouse, the Deaf & Dumb Institute in Baring Street, Millbay Laundry, Winnicott Brothers ironmongers in Ebrington Street and Stuart Photo Services in Prince Rock.

Meanwhile, a number of other new stores were opening their doors: in May Messers EJC and TH Penwill, directors of the long-established wine and spirit importers, Poppleston & Co. started trading in the City Centre again, after a twelve-year absence and in premises that were only yards from their pre-war base. John Hawkins' fabric store soon followed suit, in Cornwall Street, along with the GEC (General Electric Company premises at the bottom end of the new development, Union Street, and Boots the Chemist, at the top end, on the corner of Old Town Street and New George Street.

The new Boots and the old Drake Circus, with its fondly remembered illuminated Guinness Clock.

For all that Royal Parade was beginning to look like the finished article there were still a number of Blitz survivors.

Apart from the Trustees Savings Bank, the GEC building and the new Gas Board premises, there was no notable work being carried out west of the Co-op at the bottom of Royal Parade.

Meanwhile, south of Royal Parade, most of the major work was concentrated around the former Princess Square, where there were still a number of pre-war buildings as well as post-war pre-fabricated Nissen huts.

The two schemes progressing here, alongside the newly emerging extension to Armada Way, were the new NAAFI (Navy, Army and Air Force Institute) and Barclays Bank buildings.

With architectural echoes of Norwich Town Hall (and Stockholm Town Hall before that), work had begun on the NAAFI in 1949. Designed by EM Joseph the red-brick building represented a marked departure from the Portland stone finishes being applied elsewhere in the new City Centre, but it was to be complemented by the Roman Catholic church of Christ the King on the other side of Armada Way.

The Stockholm reference is an interesting one as the Swedes had long admired the work of Patrick Abercrombie and in December 1945 the planning professor had visited new housing projects in Sweden, and was particularly taken by the 'Star Flats' being favoured there.

Above: *Clearance work commences on the west end of town.* Right: *Nissen hut shops in Princess Square.*

Above: *Part of Notte Street is cleared for the new NAAFI Building* (right top and bottom).

The first phase of the Barclay's Bank development goes up across the road from the new NAAFI.

'These designs found their way into the Plymouth reconstruction programme, with the Star block next to the NAAFI being one of the best examples.' (Hobbins)

In the event the NAAFI building was opened in the summer of 1952 – on Friday 18 July - with Princess Margaret cutting the ribbon.

In September, as the line of Armada way stretched ever southwards towards the Hoe, work began on Sir Edward Maufe's plans for extending the Naval War Memorial on the edge of the Hoe Promenade. Paton-Watson had always intended this to be the crowning glory of Armada Way - it was absolutely central to the line of that great north/south axis and now it was possible to see how the engineer's vision would soon be realised.

A small section of Citadel Road and most of Windsor Place were about all that now stood in the way of a clear line of sight south of Notte Street, while on the north side there were still a number of Nissen hut-housed temporary shops as well as a few Blitz survivors in what was left of Westwell Street.

In October the first phase of the new Barclays building was completed. At the time they had no idea how long it would be before they would be permitted to complete the building - it turned out to be almost five years.

Top: *Armada Way stretches south.* Below: *Notte Street moves east.*

Martin's Bank appears on the corner of Armada Way and Cornwall Street.

Originally the plan had been to create a banking precinct in the reconstruction area and one of the businesses that had been temporarily housed in Westwell Street was Martin's Bank, which had been based in George Street before the war – they'd opened a branch there at the beginning of 1939. Their new premises opened on another corner of Armada Way (the north western junction with Cornwall Street) in the second half of the 1950s, by which time various other key corners of the new City Centre had either been put in place or set in motion.

It's interesting to note that the name Armada Way had not been the unanimous choice of the City Council: ultimately approved by a 22-18 majority vote, other suggestions had included Phoenix Way, Hoegate and Churchill Way. There was a clear logic to all the alternatives, but as Paton-Watson's proud new thoroughfare was being laid out towards the Hoe in the wake of the Allied success in the Second World War and as the Hoe is reputed to be where Drake played his famous game of bowls before setting sail to defeat the Spanish Armada (thereby foiling the last serious attempt to invade our shores) then there was something more emotive perhaps about

the Armada association. Doubtless the fact that both the Armada Tercentenary Memorial and Drake's Statue were to be found at either side of the Hoe end of Armada Way played some part as well, as did the fact that Lady Astor deliberately led the wartime dancing on the Hoe, beneath Boehm's defiant figure of Drake.

The push to complete Armada Way by the summer of 1953 was doubtless a keen objective of it's architect, Paton-Watson, as in June, as the newly elected President of the Institute of Municipal Engineers, he hosted a visit to Plymouth of delegates from the Institute's annual conference that was being held in Torquay.

His peers from around the country were mightily impressed with what they found here:

'The City Council and the City Engineer have done a wonderful job and if they continue as they are going Plymouth will be one of the finest cities in the country ...' said Swindon's Borough Engineer, J Ackroyd.

'The thing that astonishes me, knowing something of the difficulties of working conditions during the post-war years and understanding something of the difficulties of obtaining Government permission for materials,' volunteered the West Bromwich Borough Engineer, H Schofield, *'is the tremendous progress compared with some of the other blitzed cities.'*

It was a sentiment echoed by the Mayor of West Bromwich, H Sower; *'Plymouth has made the speediest and most complete recovery so far from war damage.'*

While JC Britton, who chaired a number of committees of Ilkeston Town Council, made the wistful observation that *'at a previous cost in life, Plymouth was given a wonderful opportunity, which it has exploited to the full.'*

Clearly the visiting officials were impressed and while Plymouth people and local businesses may have been frustrated by the delays in getting licences and materials, the comments of these distinguished visitors in the local press put a lot of these concerns in context.

As Dr Bevan, Dover's Borough Engineer put it: *'We look with admiration and envy on the tremendous steps you have made in rebuilding your city. I wish we could say the same in Dover.'*

To the outsider, less than ten years after the end of the war, Plymouth looked very state of the art, with Royal Parade a bright, broad new boulevard that had no equal anywhere in England.

The north side of Royal Parade is almost complete, New George Street is filling up and Cornwall Street is well under way, while a significant part of the old market still stands.

Above: *The top end of New George Street, with Moons.* Bottom: *Top end of Cornwall Street.*

Around the same time as this great number of green-eyed Borough Engineers from around the country descended on the City news filtered through that Plymouth had been granted another £216,450 worth of building licences, including those for Donald Hamilton (a block of six shops on the corner of Cornwall Street/Armada Way), Horne Brothers (New George Street/Armada Way), and Costers (New George Street).

Former Lord Mayor (1949-50), Frank Leatherby, one of the Costers directors announced that the aim would be to build a store, suitably modernised and similar to their pre-war premises: *'We shall still cater for the same class of trade, with a major portion of the building devoted to men's wear.'*

At that time the well-known and expanding (they had bought out Bowden's in Russell Street and Derries in Cornwall Street in 1952) local business had been operating out of a number of different temporary homes around the City Centre. The firm had been set up some sixty years earlier by Alfred Coster, a former manager with John Yeo & Co., in Bedford Street. Alfred had died in 1906, without an heir and the business would appear to have been bought by Edward Leatherby and his wife Bessie Prynn, a daughter of the Devonport family of tailors.

By a curious quirk of fate, on 8 September 1953, just weeks after work began on the new Costers building, the impressive new John Yeo & Co. department store opened on Royal Parade. It now meant that there were only two gaps left on the northern side of Royal Parade to be filled, respectively, by Spooners and Pophams, the former being at least 18 months from a projected opening date.

By now most of the big players looking to open in the City Centre had arrived, although there was still a lot of work to be done before the grand vision of the Co-operative building was completed, while both Marks & Spencer and Woolworths were scheduled for expansion. British Home Stores and Littlewood's were the only two really big chains stores still waiting, frustrated, in the wings.

Having said that, there were still dozens of smaller firms waiting to start building and, infuriatingly for the majority of them, it looked like they were going to have to wait at least another three or four years Meanwhile, among those other new projects given the go-ahead in the summer of 1953, in the industrial area, were Auto Factors at Cattedown, and the Cattedown Social Club.

It's worth noting that not all voices were as one over the new City Centre. Speaking at the Ministry of Housing and Local Government inquiry into the Plan for Plymouth at Devonport Guildhall, CR Milford, the manager of the Plymouth branch of the Halifax Building Society said that he thought that the proposed shopping centre was too big. He said that someone 'who could be regarded as an expert' had suggested to him that the amount of shops planned would be adequate for a population of a million, four times more than the population of the City.

There were also concerns that because of the level of ground rents, rates and building costs, many smaller, pre-war local businesses were being forced to relinquish opportunities of continuing in the City Centre. The result of this was that more and more national chain stores would move into the City Centre, at the expense of a bit of local character.

Solicitor HJW Ruse was further concerned that a number of old City Centre pubs were being lost without adequate replacement, although it's interesting to note that Plymouth's restaurant facilities were already edging close to what they had been before the war. As of October 1953, and the opening of the café in John Yeo's, there were now three on Royal Parade, with Dingles having recently opened a 300-seater. There were also plans for an even larger facility in Spooner's, while Fuller's were in the process of building in New George Street as was the Tudor restaurant in Ebrington Street, with additional outlets on the way from Goodbodys, Lyons and the Co-op in the final phase of their development.

There was further criticism voiced by Group V (a body of local architects) that the new City Centre looked better from the air - in other words, as it would appear on the drawing-board. They felt that it presented a dull vista, rather than an inspiring view and that by adopting a formal pattern plan, the full possibilities of the site had been ignored: monotony had replaced variety and bleak solidarity had replaced vitality.

Flexibility, they claimed, had no part in the present plan.

Another view was expressed by a local artist, James Aitchell: *'I think it is probable that posterity will give its verdict of the new Plymouth. Indeed, I would go farther and say that the planners and builders of Plymouth are creating not only a new city, but a new era in urban architecture.'*

Top: *The Pophams/Lloyds building completes Royal Parade.*
Bottom: *Work begins on the new Pannier Market.*

Curiously enough, one building that pre-dated all this post-war development and, yet architecturally at least, sat very comfortably within the new landscape, was the Royal Cinema. Built on the site of Foulston's impressive 1813 Theatre Royal (which was demolished in 1937 to make way for a building more suited to the modern world of entertainment), the Royal Cinema was one of 45 designed by William Riddle Glenn for the Associated British Cinema (ABC) chain. Today only half of them survive, and only four, including the 1938 Plymouth building, are hanging on as cinemas.

With the exception of the old Bank building (now a pub) and Derry's Clock tower, all the other surviving pre-war structures have gone. Most, like the shell of Foulston's original Athenaeum building, went in the fifties, although the Lockyer Tavern stood until 1984, two years after Plymouth's new Theatre Royal opened, to allow the Bank building to be extended as a public house.

This page and opposite: *the area around the ABC Royal, Derry's Clock and the old bank and Lockyer Tavern a rare pocket of Blitz survivors destined to last into the twnety-first century.*

Above and inset: Mutley Plain in 1946, enjoying a brief period as the City's premier shopping area.

THE SHOPPING EXPERIENCE

While the main shopping centres of the Three Towns – Plymouth, Stonehouse and Devonport – all took a tremendous battering during the war, Mutley Plain came through bombing comparatively unscathed. As a consequence, the busy arterial strip enjoyed a brief period as Plymouth's premier shopping centre. Aligned along the principal north-south route into and out of the City Centre, Mutley had largely developed in the late-nineteenth century and with heavy population concentrations to the east and west was already a thriving retail area. The major banks – Lloyds, Barclays, National Provincial, Midland and the Plymouth & South Devon Savings Bank – all had branches there. So too did WH Smith, while the Co-operative occupied a large number of premises, as did furnishers Charles Harding and grocers Dilleigh's. Boots the Chemists, along with Timothy Whites & Taylors, and CJ Park all represented the pharmacy trade. There were butchers (Parker, Milican, Dewhurst, Lidstone, Hendy, Nicholls, Walke, and Quick), bakers (Stephens, Bedford, and Goodbody), fishmongers (Mock, Cload, Weeks), fuiterers (Finnemore, Harvey, Peraton), launderers (Millbay, Bellom, and Without Delay) wine merchants (Ellery), wireless outlets (Arthur Brand, City Radio), tobacconists (Pengelly, Matthews, Hadley, Snell, and Garmstone), as well as numerous hairdressers, dentists, opticians and shoe shops and a cycle shop, perambulator provider, motor showroom and so on.

Dilleigh's had an advantage over some of their competitors as they had already had a base on Mutley Plain before the war.

Among the properties that Dingles temporarily relocated to were two large villas north of Mutley Plain – Ingleside (top left) and Carlton (bottom left and right, inside). Others made use of hastily erected Nissen huts set up at various points around the City Centre.

Almost all of these businesses were still operating on Mutley Plain after the war, but they were soon joined by branches of some of the larger city centre stores that had been displaced by the bombing. Dingles moved their drapery departments into Nos1 & 3, 12, 62, 65 & 68 Mutley Plain, while Pophams opened clothing and fabric outlets in No2 and 4 on the other side of the road. John Yeo's, meanwhile, managed to acquire Nos 13, 54 & 56 to conduct a similar trade, with Spooners opening one of their many immediate post-war retail outlets on Townsend Hill, just up from another branch of Dingles.

The property chase on the Plain was by no means restricted to the drapery departments of the City Centre heavyweights, as a number of National chains sought and found suitable premises on the strip, among them: H Samuel (jeweller), Currys (cycles), Saxone (shoes), Hector Powe (tailor), and Bateman (optician).

All of this increased retail activity of course prompted a higher local footfall for Mutley's local cinema, the Belgrave, as well as the Empire Billiard Club, the Mutley Assembly Rooms (a favourite among the dancing fraternity) and the three pubs, the Hyde Park, Fortescue, and Nottingham.

And it wasn't just Mutley Plain itself as North Hill, Townsend Hill and Thorn Park were among the other peripheral areas to suddenly find themselves pushed into the commercial spotlight. Generally speaking the bigger the business the more likely it was to have been scattered across the city and this was particularly true of the department stores for whom splitting up into specialised isolated units was always going to be easier than for the more homogenous type of trader.

Of course, while finding out-of-area shops and buildings was useful, for those who needed larger premises, there were other solutions on hand for those who could operate in smaller spaces, or indeed those who were desperate to retain a city centre presence, no matter how cramped the unit, hence the demand for the many Nissen huts that swiftly spread across the rubble-strewn hinterland like a series of corrugated scars marking those bombs sites that were relatively low on the potential redevelopment list.

South of the line designated for Royal Parade saw the highest concentration, around Princess Square, west of Westwell Street and on the site that would ultimately be occupied by the Civic Centre. Another busy site was that opposite the Central Library.

Top: *Typical Children's Wear section with an almost total lack of corporate branding.*
Bottom: *Dingles' temporary grocery store in Westwell Street.*

Clockwise from top left: *The mural painting of the view from St Teresa's. Frederick Cook's view of Polperro, painted for Dingles; two views of the Pilgrim Fathers' departure, painted for the new Co-operative buildings.*

No matter how successful any of these alternative outlets were for the local retailers though, none were as attractive as the proposition of having a shiny new shop in town.

As the frustrating forties came to a close and the first new post-war Portland-stone-and-glass stores started to appear in Plymouth City Centre there was a subtle but significant trend that insinuated itself across the interiors of a number of the new developments - that of the mural.

The phenomenon appears to have gained momentum during wartime, British Restaurants notably had commissions from a number of well-known artists, including Mary Adshead, who, after the war painted a stunning scheme for Selfridges in London, and many murals in this area including Plymstock Church, the Barley Sheaf pub and the Council House (the latter two both in 1961). Mary's father, incidentally, was Stanley Adshead, an architect and professor at Liverpool University and an acquaintance of Patrick Abercrombie (they co-authored a survey of the Thames in 1929), Stanley also laid out Plymouth's first large twentieth-century housing estate at Swilly.

At the forefront of Plymouth's post-war mural painting was Vincent Bennett (a jazz musician/artist/art teacher) who, in the mid-late forties painted several, including one in a café in the Octagon, and another in a Union Street pub, the Sydenham (now the Clipper see page 166), but it was in the wake of the 1951 Festival of Britain that the fashion really seems to have taken hold.

Ushering in an era described as 'bringing art to the people' there were one or two truly massive murals painted as part of the Festival, with the South Bank Exhibition alone including around 100 large works by almost as many artists - a good number of them in restaurants scattered around the exhibition area.

In Plymouth the colourful phenomenon found a ready home inside the mono-coloured stone clad structures that were arising from the ashes: among the most prominent examples, the Barbican mural in the new Dingles' bakery – St Teresa's in Ebrington Street – which opened, ahead of any new City Centre buildings, in January 1950.

Then, when Dingles' main new department store opened the following year there were several murals by Polperro-based artist Frederick Cook on show in the stairwells. Prior to that, however, in June 1951, neighbouring shoe store, Dolcis had opened and unveiled its 16x8ft mural of a Westcountry beach scene, by Plymouth School of Art student, Merrill Williams.

Top: The mural in Dolcis children's department.
Middle and bottom: Two trade-based murals from the new Co-operative buildings in Royal Parade.

71

Artwork wasn't the only area that retailers looked to when it came to the edification of the general public: for many years some of the major players had looked to books to help attract, entertain and educate their customer. The Co-operative had been hiving off a percentage of its annual turnover for education purposes since it started in the City back in the 1860s, while for some time a number of notable high-street retailers had their own subscription libraries, like Harrods in London and WH Smiths and Boots across the country generally.

It was Florence Boot, wife of Jesse Boot (the son of Boot's founder John Boot), who instigated the Boots' Book-Lending service back in 1898 and in the early days all stock was second-hand. However, in a very short time that all changed and by 1903 (seven years before Plymouth's first purpose-built public library opened in Tavistock Road) almost half of the 300 Boots stores across the country had their own subscription library. By 1920 half a million customers had enlisted and by the end of the thirties Boots were buying 1,250,000 books a year, giving them considerable influence in the book-publishing world.

After the war the new stores in both Plymouth and Southampton were equipped with state-of-the-art libraries, however, they were destined to be short-lived.

The Plymouth Boots, on the corner of New George Street and Old Town Street, opened during Coronation month, June 1953, and at that time Plymouth Central Library was still little more than a burnt-out shell.

Eleven months later, Princess Margaret unveiled a tablet commemorating the beginning of the reconstruction and early in 1956 the revamped library was ready to reopen, thereby putting pressure on the viability of Boots' subscription library. Add to that the growing popularity – and availability – of the paperback and the increasing preparedness for central government to invest in public libraries and it's no surprise to find that the WH Smith chain decided to close their libraries in 1961 and four years later Boots came to the same conclusion, the last Boots' Booklovers Libraries closing in February 1966.

Top: *Boots Booklovers Library.* Bottom: *Library staff, Plymouth, 31 October 1955; l-r Maureen Coggin, Christine Court, Mrs Stella White, Margaret Friswell, Jean Phillips and behind her, Jean Blatchford. Opposite page: Norwich Union Building and Boots by night. Note the traffic lights.*

Inside Curry's at Christmas.

Just as royalty could sometimes be prevailed upon to open civic buildings, so the Lord Mayor and local and national celebrities were, from time to time, engaged to open commercial concerns. With so many official openings happening in the city, there was, inevitably, a steady trickle of film stars, pop stars and radio and television personalities arriving in Plymouth to perform the ceremonial ribbon snipping.

As well as the actresses already referred to (Mercy Haystead and Anne Crawford) we had, among others, the former Irish middleweight boxing champion Eamonn Andrews, opening Curry's new retail outlet in Armada Way, on 2 April 1954. Over an eight-year period Andrews had graduated from boxer to radio sports journalist to national television star, and although television was then yet to make a major impact here, Eamonn was already a star as host of the popular What's My Line panel game. The even more famous and longer-running series, This Is Your Life, would start in the following year.

Meanwhile, a year or two later, Pye recording artist Petula Clark deputised for label-mate Lonnie Donegan at the opening of Harold Jones' new Radio and TV shop in Cornwall Street, where there was plenty of Pye equipment with television sales (and rentals) now starting to boom.

2 April 1954, boxing and television star Eamonn Andrews opns the new Curry's store in Armada Way.

Top: The new double-headed shaver is tested. Bottom: Petula Clark opens Harold Jones' new TV shop in Cornwall Street - Harold is pictured above the scissors, with his daughters, Sue and Marjorie either side of

The not so gradual ascendency of television was one of the major elements highlighting the distinction between pre- and post-war Britain. Another was the gradual demise of horse-drawn traffic. Although few, if any, private individuals or private-hire companies called upon the services of those well-loved beasts of burden after the war, their use by certain commercial concerns, who needed to make journeys that involved a great deal of stopping and starting, continued well into the fifties.

The Co-op, although foremost among the major horse-drawn hauliers were, nevertheless, introducing more and more electric- and petrol-driven vehicles into their fleets. In September 1951 the Society pulled up its last horse-drawn grocery vehicle and in March 1952 they called in their last quadruped-powered greengrocery cart. That just left the bakery division with its one-horse-power service, and in February 1954 that too was taken off the road. The old stables at Peverell were converted for storage space, and thus ended an era mourned by many, especially those roundsmen who liked to share a tipple with their customers around the festive period.

Of course, therein lay a tenuous clue to one of the last regular employers of equine energy … the breweries. Dray horses were, for years, kept on, latterly only for special occasions: their main use was as slow-moving, hard-working creatures who hauled beer barrels in the days when there were considerably more little pubs dotted around the Three Towns, a good number of which sourced their beer from local breweries – of which there were many – and rather than stop/start a motor engine, it was easier to keep the horses waiting, until instructed to move on.

Top left: Roundsman Douglas Robertson leads the last horse-drawn grocery cart back to Peverell. Middle: 27 February 1954 the last Co-op horse is pensioned off. Bottom: May 1950, Wesley Place, Peverell: Ernest Wright, in flat cap, with Prince and Reg Pengelly (van boy), and Jim Wright. Above: Mabel Easton, Mrs Nicholls and others outside the Ship Inn (Watering Hole) on the Barbican.

Above and right: Douglas Robertson's Co-operative Society grocery van. *Top right:* Co-op coal truck.

Notwithstanding the demise of the horse and cart the travelling roundsman was a common and, for many, an essential feature of post-war life. As new the estates sprang up around the city the pattern was invariably the same, houses first, shops, community centres and public transport networks second. All of a sudden a generation of Plymothians who were used to living in tight-knit communities with corner shops at the end of nearly ever terrace found themselves living, albeit in more comfortable conditions, in sprawling urban environments, a long way from the nearest general store and a bit of a hike to the nearest bus stop.

The Co-operative Society was well placed to reach out into these new communities, although they were by no means the only ones operating in that field. However, with dozens of branches already dotted around the patch, they had an in-built advantage. What is more, their whole ethos, with all profits, apart from the customers' 'divi' being readily reinvested, they were in a cash-rich position and easily able build anew on the fledgling estates. And, in the event of there being no suitable short-term site to develop, they could convert one of the new domestic dwellings, as they did at Ernesettle. That and the decision to start introducing self-service, in 1948, kept the Society ahead of the game.

Top: *21 July 1946, Leslie Burnett and Harry Osmond exchanging Uglows bread for coupons.* Bottom left and right: *Jack Glanville and assistants working for Pearks of Devonport.*

Clockwise from top left: *The Co-op open a branch in a Cornish unit house in Ernesettle; the new, 1950, Co-op warehouse on North Quay; the Society's Radnor Dairy; a new bakery van.*

Above: *Frank Chapman's Embankment Road garage (removed in 1955 for road widening).* Right: *Chapman's Service Station at Compton with modern pumps.*

ON THE ROAD

At the very beginning of the twentieth century there were less than 8,000 motor vehicles on British roads, and motoring was largely regarded as a hobby for the well-to-do. The number of car registrations, however, grew quite steadily up to the outbreak of the Second World War and yet by the end of the war over 90 per cent of households were still without a car. With petrol rationing still in force in 1946 there was little to encourage motoring in the post-war world, and yet within a couple of years the number of private vehicles on British roads broke the two million mark and by 1955 that figure had doubled.

The boom period was good news to all local garage proprietors, especially those who already had well-established businesses.

Frank Chapman had established his garage at Lipson Vale in 1934 and built up a small chain with premises at Wolseley Road, Compton and the Embankment.

William Folland started his business just dealing in oil, in Florence Place, off Embankment Road in 1892, later moving into a site that included the old toll houses for the Embankment and Laira Bridge.

Meanwhile, Gilbert Reed's Cobourg Street enterprise had been started in 1924, and two years earlier FG Barton had expanded the business he began in Torquay, by opening a garage on the corner of Mutley Plain and Ford Park – in 1930 he opened a new, purpose-built, garage and showroom further along the Plain.

Folland's Garage, just off Laira Bridge on the Plymouth side.

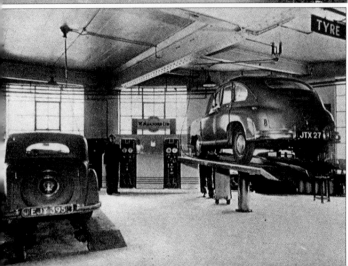

In 1950 Mumfords celebrated their half century, William Mumford having started out working on horse-drawn vehicles at the dawn of the twentieth century.

He moved on to motor cars eight years later and in 1946 they became the first body factors outside of Rolls-Royce's own factories to be allowed to work on those vehicles. Their substantial premises in St Andrew Street happily survived the war.

Other eminent names on the scene at that time included Humm's (who had opened brand new premises just before the war, on the corner of Princess Square and Westwell Street), Vosper's, Allen's, M Thomas Motors, Pike's, Andrew's, and perhaps the daddy of them all - Mumford's.

William Mumford had started out repairing horse-drawn vehicles at the turn of the century –1900 – in Glanville Street. Three years later he moved into Ebrington Street and in 1908 started working on motor cars, indeed he assembled the first car body in the West of England.

A keen exponent of new developments in transport Mumford was a big fan of Louis Bleriot, the man who made the first crossing of the English Channel in a heavier-than-air craft, in 1909, and so it was that Mumford constructed a copy of the Bleriot machine, albeit without an engine.

Mumford also manufactured the bodywork for the first motor-buses to operate in Plymouth, between Derry's Clock and Crownhill. And they produced bodywork for charabancs and taxi cabs.

In 1915 they moved into premises in Salisbury Road and soon afterwards began selling cars: the first being the Briton which retailed at £220. And therein lay the key to the post-war car boom, for over thirty years later Ford released their latest affordable machine, the Ford Popular with a retail price of just £275.

Despite the exigencies of war Mumford's city centre base in St Andrew Street was able to carry on after the war, although they lost their showroom in Old Town Street. The business had an interesting post-war boost when, in 1946 they became the first body factors to be allowed to work on Rolls-Royce vehicles, outside of the Rolls-Royce factory.

Not that there was a great demand locally for such work, as Plymouth has never been a particularly affluent city, however, in the late-forties and early-fifties there was still plenty of work in the Dockyard and on the housing estates and in the city centre, there was more building work than ever before. Add the new factories into the financial equation and it's easy to see how the motor car was becoming a more viable option for many.

PHONE **4292**
FOR
RADIO DIRECTED
SUPERCABS
DAY & NIGHT SERVICE
33 St. Andrew St. Plymouth.

We Lead - - Others Follow

**PLYMOUTH LUXICAB
HIRE SERVICE**

Proprietor : C. R. HUDSON

Phone 2838 (20 Lines) Phone 2838

LUGGAGE FREE   NO EXTRAS
Special Quotations for 25 miles or over

Top: Folland's fleet of wedding cars. Above: Taxis outside North Road Station. Right; Saunder's taxi 1949.

A logical progression for some of the local garages, because they had the wherewithal to service and repair vehicles, was to move into the world of taxi cabs, the provision of vehicles for weddings, funerals and private hire or self-drive (there were few national firms). One or two of the taxi firms - among them Supercabs, Luxicabs and Les Rowe's Priority Taxi Service - advertised themselves as offering a day and night service.

Charges were fairly consistent and by the mid-fifties the standard charge for any journey less than a mile was two shillings (10p) with each extra third of a mile ('or part thereof') adding another sixpence (2.5p) to the fare. For bookings involving more than two people there was an extra sixpence per person and the charge for waiting for a customer was four shillings an hour. There was also an additional charge (3d) for each extra item of luggage that couldn't be carried inside the cab.

But it was by no means a universal service and with drink-driving restrictions only going so far as to apprehend those who were caught attempting to drive while *under the influence of drink or a drug to such an extent as to be incapable of having proper control of the vehicle*, in other words there was no legal limit, there were plenty of drivers who were prepared to court danger.

Interior of Ivan Lang's garage/workshop.

Top: *Saltash Ferry landing vehicles in Cornwall.* Bottom: *Loading cars on the Saltash side.*

Despite the best endeavours of the enemy to damage local communication links, both the Torpoint and Saltash ferries ran an uninterrupted service throughout the war.

The Saltash service at that time was reliant on two floating bridges brought into action in 1927 and 1933 respectively.

The first was a little larger than its 16-year-old predecessor, which was kept in reserve until 1933 when it was sold to serve on the Fal as the King Harry Ferry (as it transpired, however, it was too big for that crossing and soon afterwards sank on her way to a ship breaker in Wales).

The new vessel had been manufactured in Kingswear by Philip & Son and could, initially, accommodate three rows of fifteen cars – but in 1938 it was cut down the middle and extended by six feet.

The second ferry came from Southampton, courtesy of Messrs Thorneycroft, and was officially brought into service on Boxing Day 1933. Like its companion this ferry had a red/brown band running around the vessel for a few feet above the waterline and was topped out in a neutral buff colour with black funnelling. This second new ferry subsequently shared duties with its companion, and the two switched duties twice a year; between them they ran throughout the thirties, forties and fifties.

The service operated on the hour and half hour from Saltash and quarter to and quarter past the hour on the Devon side. The last ferry from the St Budeaux side left Saltash Passage at 11.15pm each evening, and if you missed that it was a seven-hour wait until the service started up again.

Charges were 1/6d (7p) for cars and 10 shillings (50p) for coaches: pedestrians paid 2d, unless they were from Saltash in which case they travelled free.

Almost certainly the most notable passenger in the post-war period was the young Princess Elizabeth, who began a two-day tour of Cornwall on 21 October 1949 and came to Plymouth on 22 October 1949 to commemorate the start of the rebuilding of St Andrew's Church.

Although there was some wartime damage to the Torpoint Ferries, the service ran on a similar basis, except that it started slightly earlier in the morning, 5.30am, and ended a little later in the evening – there was a midnight ferry out of Devonport. Traditionally the busier of the two services, the Torpoint crossing was, furthermore, regularly served, from the thirties onwards, by two 36-car ferries between 7.45am and 9.45am, which meant that this was a fifteen-minute, rather than a thirty-minute service, provided, of course, that there were no queues! There was also an hourly night service.

The construction of new housing estates in Torpoint, from 1945/6 onwards – Hamoaze and Cremyll – and from 1952/3 at Queens Park estate, inevitably put further pressure on this busy crossing.

This page: left - top and bottom: *the Torpoint Ferry in action.*
Above: *Queues snake back to the Ferry House Hotel.*

Mount Gould coach trip party with Colin Brown, Norman Truscott, Jack Ellacott, John Graham, Jim Basset, Flo Babb, Margery Page, Rev Andrew Crawford, Eve Brown (née Adamson), John Edwards, Mrs Andrews, Marie Prickett (Colllns), Margaret Richards, Miss Ellacott, Mr Ellacott, Muriel Bennet, Hilary Larson, Mrs Crawford, Peter Conway, Eileen Baker (Gerry), Frances Brown, Harry Hodge, Jeanne Conway, Mavis Pruce (Gerry), Beryl Sweet, John Sweet, John Cloake, Jill Basset (Edwards), Vera Brooks, Roger Larson, Marie Weaver, Mike Beavil, Max Toys, Mr Radmore and Dave Barry.

As did the increasing numbers of people in their private cars looking to take day trips across the Tamar. For most people though in that immediate post-war period, day trips were synonymous with coach outings.

These day trips were especially significant when set alongside the statistic revealed in a 1949 nationwide survey: to whit, almost 50 per cent of British adults had not had a holiday away from home that year, but just over half of those stay at homers had been on at least one day trip. This, of course, suggested that almost a quarter of the population had no sort of away-day break at all, despite the legislation of the previous year – the Holidays with Pay Act – which entitled every employed adult to two weeks' paid leave every year.

Not surprisingly perhaps the more affluent you were the more likely you were to take a holiday: however with post-war hardship still a reality for many, the finding that something like a quarter of the adult population, mainly the older generation, had not taken a holiday for many years was not altogether surprising. Neither was the finding that something like 4 per cent of those who did take holidays, stayed with friends and family rather than opting for a hotel or guest house. As for destinations, almost all holidays were taken (98 per cent) in this country, and two-thirds of them were by the seaside. Plymouth, being a seaside town, had invested heavily in marketing itself as a tourist destination and in the absence of a sandy beach, had created the Hoe Lido in the mid-thirties to complement the other waterside facilities between Fisher's Nose and Rusty Anchor.

Additionally there were the ferry crossings to Cremyll and Turnchapel and Oreston, but more significantly perhaps Plymouth had long since marketed itself as the Centre of A Hundred Tours and here it was that the coach operators came into their own:

'The West of England with its gloriously wooded hills and valleys, unsurpassed coastal scenery and quaint old villages, has much to commend it,' ran the advertising copy on a Western National advertisement. It was followed by the line 'Western National Services will help to make your holiday enjoyable.' The company, based throughout the forties in their pre-war home in Whimple Street, offered regular daily omnibus services and coaches for private hire, as did the Co-operative, who had a travel office in Raleigh Street, and 'the firm with the personal touch', the Embankment Motor Company, who were also still in pre-war premises in Westwell Street.

Coach parties assemble outside the Corn Exchange.

EMBANKMENT
MOTOR COMPANY (PLYMOUTH) LTD
33 WESTWELL STREET ◆ COACH TOURS
"The Firm with the Personal Service"

MOTOR COACHES
for **PRIVATE HIRE**

SPORTING FIXTURES ★ SOCIAL VISITS
THEATRE PARTIES ★ WORKS OUTINGS
----- ANY SIZE PARTY ------- ANY DISTANCE -----

*For First Class Service
at a Reasonable Charge*

Please address enquiries to:

EMBANKMENT
MOTOR COMPANY ● (PLYMOUTH) LTD.
33 WESTWELL STREET
PLYMOUTH
Phone 5749

SEE THE BEST OF THE WEST
BY . . .
THE
WESTERN NATIONAL
OMNIBUS COMPANY LIMITED

The West of England, with its gloriously wooded hills and valleys, unsurpassed coastal scenery and quaint old villages, has much to commend it. "Western National" Services will help to make your holiday enjoyable.

REGULAR DAILY OMNIBUS SERVICES
Excursions and Tours to Scenic and Historic Places
COACHES FOR PRIVATE HIRE
ROYAL BLUE Express Services to London and the South Coast

★ Address your enquiries to :—
Area Office.
**20 WHIMPLE STREET,
PLYMOUTH**
A/W 266

Travel
LAND SEA AND AIR

We shall be happy to deal with your enquiries at the
CO-OP Travel Service Office, Raleigh Street, **Plymouth**
OFF ROYAL PARADE
SUMMER TOURS—OUR COMFORTABLE and RELIABLE COACHES leave daily for all points of interest in Devon and Cornwall. There are also Extended Tours, 3—12 days. See Press Announcements & Published Schedule. Phones 2800, 3606

Top: *Vehicles of the Heybrook Bay Motor Services Company.* Below: *The end of the tram era.*

There was a fourth independent operator in the area - The Heybrook Bay Motor Services company who, in addition to their private hire and tour business, ran two bus services out of Plymouth, to Heybrook Bay and Bovisand. Based originally in their pre-war site (when they were known as the Star Motor Service) in East Street, they took a site off Treville Street when the development of New George Street saw the end of the surviving buildings around the old Market site.

In conjunction with Western National (who serviced Plymstock, Billacombe, Elburton, Oreston, Radford and Hooe) the Heybrook Bay company with their small fleet of 26-seater Bedfords were the principal providers of bus travel across the Plym. However, in December 1959, they eventually sold out to Western National and the Heybrook Bay and Bovisand runs became routes 54 and 55 respectively.

With the laying out of so many new housing estates straight after the war, there were, inevitably, a large number of new bus routes created and existing ones extended. The No.9 service, from Lower Compton and No.16 from Higher Compton, were re-routed to include Efford and new routes, 28, 34, and 35 were created to service Ham, 32 and 33 Ernesettle, 17 to King's Tamerton and 84, 84a and 84b to Whitleigh.

All of this, of course, necessitated an increase in the bus fleet and between 1946 and 1950 over 100 new Leyland buses were brought into service, as well as half a dozen Crossley machines. These latter vehicles proved disappointing, and as the general manager was keen to have an all-Leyland fleet he cancelled an order for a further 14 Crossleys and opted instead to wait another 18 months for a further delivery of Leylands.

As it happened this meant a reprieve for a couple of pre-war single decker Leyland Cubs: *'they inaugurated the service No.28 to Ham, and were the first vehicles to display "City Centre" as a substitution for the old designation "Theatre".'* (Sambourne, *Plymouth 100 Years of Street Travel*, 1972)

It had been a misnomer for some time as Foulston's old Theatre Royal had been pulled down in 1937 and it was replaced by the Royal Cinema the following year, while the Theatre Royal Hotel had been destroyed in the Blitz.

Nevertheless, the Theatre site, or at least very near it, had been one of the sites commandeered by the city as a bus terminal for out of town services in the post-war period. They also had, temporarily, used

Notte Street, Lockyer Street and, up until the construction of Bretonside at the end of the fifties, a site alongside the railway bridge that stretched across Union Street.

All the while Plymouth continued to expand. In 1950 the city swallowed up the rural hinterlands of Tamerton and Roborough and between these two well-established communities the massive new Southway Housing Estate sprang up. Service No.40 was laid on to cater for the new residents, services Nos 25 and 26 were instituted to serve the infant Manadon and Austin Farm estates.

One notable feature of the new routes, into and out of these estates, was that the roads were wider than their pre-war counterparts, and this and the fact that the city centre roads were also more generously proportioned than their predecessors meant that the vehicles using these roads could afford to be a little larger. Hence the move, in 1952, for the City Transport to enlist its first 'hybridge' double-deckers. Eight feet wide, these new Leyland monsters had a centre gangway on the upper deck and allowed for a much freer movement of passengers. They also allowed the authority to dispose of all the wartime Guys and Crossleys and achieve that all-Leyland fleet ambition.

Above: Wartime Western National bus bound for Torquay from Pound Street, with Cobourg Street School behind. Top right: Temporary bus station on the City side of the Union Street bridge. Bottom right: Buses congregate in the Guildhall Square.

Top: *Steaming over Hemerdon Bank, August 1952.* Middle: *Friary Station.*
Bottom: *King's Road Station, Devonport.*

TRAINS, BOATS & PLANES

For the best part of 100 years the most popular form of mass conveyance, certainly in terms of holiday travel, was the train and in the immediate post-war period, the Nationalisation of the Railways (1948) saw great changes in that sector, not least of which was the introduction of a uniform livery.

Although Nationalisation had been on the cards for some time GWR (Great Western Railway) had entered the post-war era in 1946 by reviving the non-stop Cornish Riviera Express, between Plymouth and Paddington and the through service from the Midlands (Wolverhampton and Birmingham) to Plymouth and Penzance.

They had also, when faced with the prospect of a coal shortage during the hard winter of 1946/7, started the process of converting from steam trains to oil-fired locos.

At the end of 1947 though it was all change as GWR, the South Devon Railway, became part of the Western Region of British Railways with effect from 1 January 1948. British Railways thus, overnight, became the greatest provider of holiday transport for most Brits and

PLYMOUTH
DELIGHTFUL CENTRE FOR HOLIDAYS
Guide free from Publicity Manager (Dept. B.R.)
TRAVEL BY TRAIN   BRITISH RAILWAYS

with Plymouth being advertised as a 'Delightful Centre for Holidays' there were plenty of takers for their offers and packages.

Typically, by the mid-fifties you could buy a 17s 6d (75p) Holiday 'Runabout' ticket that would give you seven days' unlimited rail travel to various resorts and beauty spots around Devon and Cornwall.

There was also 'The City of Plymouth Holiday Express' that covered six hundred miles of railway network in the two counties over a five-day period which ran over the two middle weeks of the school summer holidays to selected resorts – *a reserved seat guaranteed and inclusive fare very low* stated the promotional blurb.

Added to those offers there were also the regular round of half-day and cheap day excursions to most of the well-known tourist destinations in Devon and Cornwall.

Inset: *Crossing the swing bridge into Hooe.* Above: *North Road Station.*

Although most people were oblivious to the fact that they were witnessing the beginning of the end of the golden age of rail and steam transport, the situation was altogether more obvious in the world of ocean liners.

Plymouth had been a significant port of call for liner operators throughout the twenties and thirties and every year tens of thousands of passengers and hundreds of thousands of mailbags would be brought ashore by one or other of Plymouth's fleet of tenders - Sir John Hawkins, Sir Richard Grenville, Sir Walter Raleigh and Sir Francis Drake. All four of them were seconded for war service and it wasn't until October 1945 that the first of them – Sir John Hawkins – was handed back to GWR after a refit in Wales. Sir Richard Grenville was released from service that same month, and like 'Hawkins' was refitted at Penarth. Grevnille and Drake both re-entered service in 1946, January and July respectively, and then, in August, the Sir Walter Raleigh, which had been converted as a mining tender during the war, arrived back in Plymouth Sound. The homecoming, however, was but brief and the following March she ended up being sold and renamed, only to spend the next 20 years working as the tender Ingenieur Reibell in Cherbourg.

Work for the three remaining tenders was less demanding than it had been before the war as 'the liner trade was low-key compared to the halcyon years between the wars' (Kitteridge: *Plymouth – Ocean Liner Port of Call*).

Occasionally a legendary liner would stop off here, most notably the Ile de France, Liberte and De Grasse, but Millbay's primary selling point – an opportunity to shave some time off the transatlantic crossing by jumping ship in Plymouth Sound and taking the train to London, rather than waiting for the ship to sail to Southampton and completing the voyage from there – was gradually losing out to the increased air traffic.

Nevertheless, in 1947, a total of 66 liners landed over 110,000 mailbags and embarked or disembarked over 3,500 passengers. The following year, when the livery of the tenders changed in keeping with new owners British Railways and the previously red funnels became corporation buff, the number of mailbags more than trebled – setting a new record in the process. Remarkably that record was broken in 1949 as almost 440,000 were landed at Millbay, but it was a short-lived peak and within a few years most of the major mail contracts were being awarded to the rapidly growing airline industry.

Middle: Queen Mary in Cawsand Bay. Inset, Bing Crosby arrives at Millbay Docks c1952. Bottom: Passengers being taken out to the Bergen Line's Venus, with Blue Star Liner Uruguay in the middle and Union Castle Liner far right.

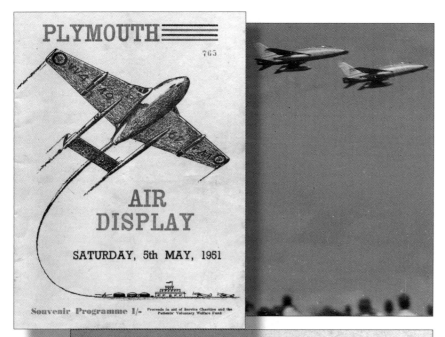

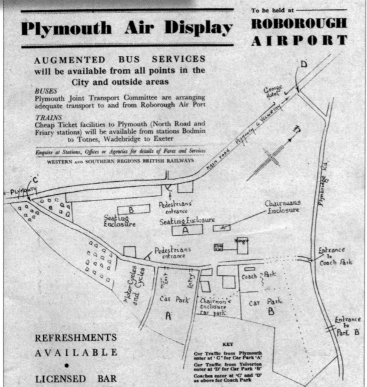

The sad part of this being that Plymouth itself had never really embraced the idea of an airport as enthusiastically as it might have done. The authors of the 1943 Plan for Plymouth had been aware of the potential, but hadn't exactly pushed for it.

They acknowledged the *'possibility of the development of a seaplane base'* but said that it *'requires the careful exploration and consideration by experts.'*

They did however identify two sites:

'The Sound, where civil aviation might conflict with the RAF Station at Mount Batten;' and *'St. John's Lake, between Mount Edgcumbe and Torpoint, where, by construction of a barrage at its entrance into the Hamoaze, a very usefully sized lake could be obtained at all states of the tide with runways of over 1,000 yards in each wind direction.'*

But they certainly didn't sound all that keen and their concluding caveat said it all: *'It should be remembered, however, that the high ground and promontories surrounding these tidal areas do not make them ideal for these purposes, and that there will be competition for this international traffic.'*

In other words there was little appetite for Plymouth to be a major competitor. With the benefit of hindsight, it was undoubtedly wise to be cautious with regard to the flying-boat phenomenon, as just two years later the last trans-Atlantic flying-boat was withdrawn from service and the Douglas DC4 land planes led the way with their criss-crossing conquest of the globe.

However the authors of the Plymouth Plan were even more hesitant on the subject of land planes and the city:

'Whilst there will definitely be a place for the aeroplane for long-distance and light freight transport, we foresee the motor car will still be at an advantage where short and medium distances are concerned, as the impracticability of housing even quite a small plane within the confines of the average small house site, coupled with the difficulties associated in "take-off" on a limited area, would necessitate the use of a central aerodrome with the consequent loss of time spent in travel to and from. The car is the most economical and convenient form of mechanical transport, and as far as can be seen, is likely to remain so for some time.'

In other words, although they were planning to more or less double the amount of land that would sit within the city's new boundaries, they did not think there would be any place for a major airfield.

Programme, plan and photograph of the Plymouth Air Display at Roborough, May 1951.

Before the war, Roborough Aerodrome sat some four miles outside the city boundary, in 1938 Plymouth had been extended from 5,711 acres to 9,515 acres – chiefly by the absorption of parts of the old Plympton St Mary rural area, most notably the built-up areas of Crownhill and Eggbuckland. In 1951, there was a further boundary extension that saw the new line moved almost to the edge of Roborough village, bringing in the whole of the parish of Tamerton Foliot, and parts of Roborough parish, including the airport and the Glenholt estate. It meant that Plymouth was now some 4,000 acres bigger than Exeter and, with over 200,000 residents, was around three times the size in terms of population and yet still information about the airport facility was conspicuously absent from the list of local amenities in the annual tourist guides.

Essentially, however, the airfield at Roborough had already been eclipsed by that of Exeter. Opened in 1937, by which time there were 128 licensed civilian aerodromes operating in Britain, Exeter was one of 32 sites that had customs facilities, which, according to the Air Ministry, officially classed it as an Airport.

At least six years younger than Plymouth, Exeter became the RAF's Sector Station during the war, which meant that it controlled the local RAF station that was developed at Harrowbeer (Yelverton) and not Plymouth.

On 1 January 1947 Exeter was transferred to the Ministry of Civil Aviation and although the immediate post-war period was quiet, it seemed to always stay one step ahead of Plymouth, there was even a small aircraft manufacturer (Chrislea) based there.

Back in Plymouth, there was an aero club and a model aeroplane club that met there and Roborough was open for anyone to walk in on a day to day basis – except on Air Show days – *'you could have a wander around the field and in the hangars if you asked nicely,'* recalled Jim Warwick, a former member of the Aircraft Recognition Club that met in the clubhouse there, and a future Air Training Corps Cadet.

A service courtesy of Jersey Airlines appears to have started up in the early fifties, doubtless at the same time as the Jersey to Exeter route opened in 1952, but it was all very low key.

Roborough Airport 1952, Audrey Thurlow and her friend Norah, bound for Jersey.

Children and staff from the Margaret Macmillan Nursery enjoying a blow on the Hoe.

FORTIES' AND FIFTIES' CHILDREN

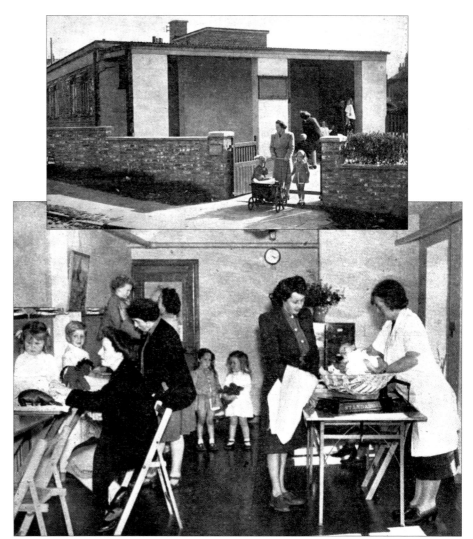

In the wake of their election success in November 1945 and in gearing up for the next polling station appeal, the Plymouth Labour party produced a Manifesto document that they entitled 'Achievement' in the early part of 1949. There had, of course, been a landslide victory for the left at both local and national level and among the various acts that had been passed in the intervening period had been the National Health Service Act, which took effect from 5 July 1948. Under the new legislation the Hospital Boards assumed control of all hospitals, but within that various duties were assigned to Local Authorities, among them the provision of ambulance services, nursing services, assistance of home helps, health centres, and maternity and child welfare clinics.

Increased demands for these services, especially the Clinic Services, saw the Council adapt and refurbish a number of gas cleansing stations, notably those at Crownhill and St Budeaux.

With regard to the creation of Health Centres, they announced the intention to erect a dozen of these, with the first scheduled to appear on the new Ham and Efford estates.

Above and inset Crownhill Clinic – *an adapted gas cleansing station.*

Top and bottom: *New schools at Ham and Efford.*

After housing, one of the most pressing issues for the local authority was undoubtedly education. It was estimated that over 7,000 school places had been wiped out by enemy action between 1940 and 1944, and in that year the passing of the Education Act succeeded in raising the school leaving age from fourteen (which is what it had been since the end of the First World War) to fifteen.

It had been the government's intention to do this in 1939, but the war had delayed matters - in Plymouth's case, just as well too, for although the new leaving age didn't become effective until 1947, between January 1944 and January 1949 the local school population grew from 19,858 to 26,305: an increase of around 6,500 places in just five years.

Small wonder therefore that the post-war period saw a massive school-building programme get underway. By 1949, in addition to the restoration of Salisbury Road School and College Road School, Keyham, four new establishments had been built and opened – Trelawney (Ham), Plym View, King's Tamerton and Montpelier.

On top of that, work was also in progress on New Montpelier, West Efford, Honicknowle Infants and Secondary (1951), and, the biggest of them all, South Crownhill (which was being designed to accommodate over 700 pupils).

Meanwhile, still on the drawing board, although the plans had been approved, were Barne Barton (1950), Knowle Fort (1952), Efford (1952), Burleigh (1955) and another 700-strong institution, Ernesettle (1952).

1952 was also the year in which, in accordance with the 1944 Act, the Local Authority published a series of public notices about those war-damaged schools that they didn't intend to rebuild and re-open: among them several that they had seriously considered restoring; King Street, Devonport; Johnston Terrace, Keyham and Palace Court, Plymouth. Among the others on whom notice was served that summer were a number of Church of England Primaries: St James the Great, St Paul's and St Stephen's; Valletort Secondary School and the primaries in East Street, Sutton Road, Union Street, Paradise Road and Wolsden Street.

The times they were undoubtedly a-changing and one other, significant element of Rab Butler's 1944 Education Act saw the introduction of another far-reaching adaptation of the English education system - the 11-plus examination.

This new, compulsory test was to be sat by all eleven-year-olds and essentially created a two-tier education system of Secondary Modern Schools, for those who didn't pass the exam, and Grammar Schools for those who did. There was, however, a third element of the new arrangement and that was the creation of the Secondary Technical School.

In the event, although most Local Education Authorities planned such schools, few councils actually built them and even at their peak less than 3 per cent of children ever attended one and admission was invariably by a separate examination and not via the 11-plus.

As it transpired, the Plymouth LEA built just one, at the very end of the fifties – Widey Technical Secondary, at Crownhill.

A large part of the resistance to this model was inspired by the Trade Unions, who considered such territory to be part of the apprenticeship system. Their resistance didn't help with the recruitment of qualified staff into this new sector, and, more significantly perhaps, their failure to really take off was, in some measure, down to the fact that Technical Schools, although perceived as a poor second to the Grammar Schools, were nevertheless one step up from a Secondary Modern and so parents sometimes pressurised their children to take the Tech exam, even though a Technical School was perhaps unsuited to their offspring.

Curiously enough the Act also allowed for the creation of Comprehensive Schools, although here there was even less take up for this initiative by LEAs around the country, and only a few were set up.

Of course there was, and always had been, another significant piece in the English education system – the Independent School. These institutions received something of a boost under the Act as the Ministry of Education (the new name for the Board of Education) created an arrangement whereby they (not the LEA) could award direct grants to the schools in return for those schools accepting a number of pupils into their fee-paying establishments on 'free places'.

Other aspects of the Act saw the introduction of compulsory daily prayers into all state schools; an enforced division between primary (5-11 years-old) and secondary schools (11-15), although this was pretty much in place already; and the introduction of free school milk. Henceforth every child in the country was entitled to a third of a pint of milk, free every day of term.

Top: *Party time at Prince Rock.* Bottom: *Hollycroft School 1949/50 with Susan Down (far left) and Edward Keast (third from the left on the middle table).*

Lipson Vale Primary which first opened its doors in September 1954.

Simon says, hide and seek, hopscotch, leap frog, piggy back, piggy in the middle, marbles, conkers, tig, tag or chase, were among the most popular and simple playground pastimes.

While square ball, rounders, cricket (often with chalked stumps on a wall), spot (kicking a football onto a 'goal' drawn on a wall), or football itself were among the easiest and most popular ad hoc playground team games.

These games and the rules and rhymes surrounding them tended to be passed down, word of mouth, by the children themselves, rather than by teachers or parents. They thus formed a key part of the learning experience: they learned how to interact with each other socially in their own time and develop some notion of 'fair play'.

Various selection processes to determine who would be 'it' in a game of tag, was integral to this development. 'Spuds Up' was a typical selection ritual, as participants stood in a line or

Top and Bottom: *Playground games.*

Left, top and bottom: *Skipping races in Verna Road, St Budeaux, with Pam Horn, Kathy Mountain, Gillian Kent.* Right, top: *Furzehill Road, 1953 Coronation Street party, with Jean Turner and Vera and Wilfred Lightfoot.* Bottom: *Skipping on the roof of Stoke Damerel School.*

a circle with their fists at waist level in front of them as someone did the rounds counting off. This would be done by hitting the players fists with their own at the same time chanting as they moved down the line: *'One potato, two potatoes, three potatoes, four, five potatoes, six potatoes, seven potatoes, more - O U T spells out.'* As the call of 'T' came down on a fist so that fist was placed behind the players back and the game carried on until there was just one spud left in the line and he or she was 'it'.

The Farmer's in his Den and In and Out of the Scottish Bluebells, were other popular primary school pastimes, but they were not necessarily exclusive to the playground or the sports hall. Most could be carried on outside of the school environment too, where streets and pavements would be pressed into action, safe in the knowledge that, outside of the main bus routes and traffic thoroughfares, there was little danger of being surprised or knocked down by a passing car.

Homage would be paid to the motor car though as old pram wheels would be rescued and fashioned, with the help of a plank or two and maybe an old soap box and a piece of steering rope, into some form of racing buggy. Brakes were more often than not, regarded as an optional extra and many's the pair of shoes that have been worn out in their stead.

Climbing trees, messing around on bomb sites, searching for shrapnel and building dens from bits of wood, metal, glass, or whatever was to hand were other character-building activities that would later be frowned upon by Health and Safety executives.

While skipping, and attempting splits, handstands and cartwheels were looked down upon by the so-called self-respecting middle classes who weren't sure that the sight of girls tucking their skirts into their knickers was an altogether decent one.

There were of course any number of different skipping games with variables including the length of rope, and the speed, and direction, in which it was turned.

A group of lithe-limbed hula-hoopping girls from Plymstock School, in 1952.

A puppet demonstration in the Library.

Indoor games included Hide and Seek, I Spy, Hunt the Thimble and pen and paper games like Noughts and Crosses, Hangman and Battleships. While other indoor activities included jigsaws, board games and model making.

In the absence of television, comics were hugely popular. The genre had taken a bit of a battering during the war, not that the appetite for the them diminished, far from it, but paper shortages, especially after Norway fell to the Germans, made their production particularly difficult. One by one various pre-war favourites simply stopped appearing - *Puck*, *Tiger*, *Tim's Weekly*, *Joker*, *Jester* and *Magic*.

A new law prohibited the launch of new regular titles, but one-offs were allowed, opening the door for The New Comics and the Jolly series.

The restrictions remained in place for some time after the war, but as the fifties dawned so did a new age of comic production, trail-blazed in April 1950 by issue No.1 of *The Eagle* with Frank Hampson's wonderfully illustrated Dan Dare the eye-catching front-page space hero.

The Eagle captured the imagination of a generation of young boys, and therein lay one of its most novel selling points, it was primarily aimed at young males. Previously comics had, for the most part, been fairly unisex in their design, but now came a significant split, one which was further accentuated by the publication of another new title in November 1951 - *Girl*.

Over the next few years *The Topper* and *The Beezer* appeared, along with *Robin* and *Jack & Jill* for the younger readers. There also appeared another new phenomenon the Library Comics. These were not actually comics that you would expect to find in proper libraries, perish the thought, rather they were pocket-sized comic books that followed the tradition of 'old story-paper serials that were reprinted in paperback format' (Gifford, *The Complete Catalogue of British Comics*, 1985) and which were known in the trade as 'libraries'.

The first off the press was *Cowboy Comics*, and it hit the newsagents at the same time as *The Eagle* – April 1950 – and its favourable reception prompted *Thriller Comics*, which came out alongside *Girl*, the following November.

Meanwhile, on the book front, 1950 saw the first in an almost annual run of Jennings adventures, Anthony Buckeridge's hugely popular schoolboy series, following in the footsteps of Charles Hamilton's (aka

Top: *Members of the Plymouth and District Model Flying Club meet in Central Park, 1947.*
Bottom: *Charlie Sells with Jim and Pete McMullin at Ernesettle c.1950.*

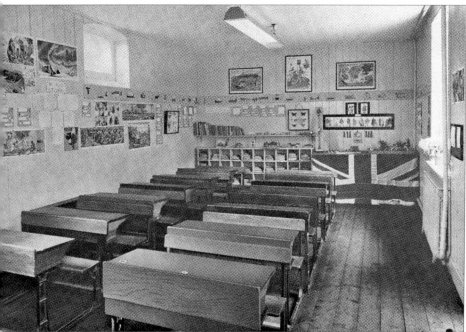

Top: Two rows of trusty old Prep school desks in Remove II. Bottom: Messrs Pearse, Erlich, Harper and Robinson make use of their microscopes as Biology enters the school curriculum.

Frank Richards) original creation for *The Magnet* comic book back in 1908 - Billy Bunter. *The Magnet* had also closed during the war and the prolific Hamilton, who had written under many pen names, was in comparative limbo for a while, until, in 1947, Billy Bunter of Greyfriars' School was published in hardback and unlocked a new phase of popularity for the Fat Owl of the Remove.

Another pre-war favourite, Richmal Crompton's enduring Just William (Brown) and his gang of Outlaws Henry, Douglas and Ginger also enjoyed a long run of hardback adventures after the war, as did WE John's fictional creation, James Bigglesworth – Biggles – who's own bunch of chums included a Ginger too, along with Algy and Bertie. For the girls there were the six early-forties tomes that made up the St Clare's series. Penned by Enid Blyton the series followed twins Pat and Isabel O'Sullivan through each year of the school experience. Blyton followed these with another series of six, published each year between 1946-51, this time chronicling the adventures of Darrell Rivers at her fictional boarding-school in Cornwall.

Enid Blyton catered for almost every age of young reader, both boys and girls, with the many adventures of Noddy and Big Ears, the fifteen separate adventures of the Secret Seven (Peter, Janet, Jack, Barbara, George, Pam and Colin) and the somewhat more celebrated collection of 21 books detailing the escapades of the Famous Five (Julian, Dick, George, Anne and Timmy the dog) delighting the baby boom generation.

This was still very much the era of the hardback book, and all new fiction and all text books were published in that format, but Allen Lane's ambitious and almost immediately successful launch of Penguin paperbacks in 1935 had already started to spark a revolution. Initially only back-catalogue titles were made available in this way – but as the attraction of the popularly priced Penguin picked up, so did the number of titles that became available in the new format.

Other advances that were to impact on spreading the word and making teaching in the classroom more interesting than ever were the increasingly affordable slide rule and the microscope: the former, fondly referred to as the 'slipstick', transformed the chores of multiplication and addition and was a boon to those previously reliant on log tables. The world of science and engineering would never be the same again. Meanwhile, the microscope, which, before the war, had been very much an expensive precision instrument used

John Dufton taking a class in the Physics Lecture room at Plymouth College.

only by boffins and other advanced research fellows, suddenly made its appearance in the classroom courtesy of Herbert J Mossien.

Mossien was the marketing manager for Bausch & Lamb, a longstanding American-based company, and it was he who saw the potential for mass-producing a microscope that could be sold into schools, thus kick-starting fresh interest in the study of a variety of subjects, most notably Biology.

Plymouth College was among the local pioneers with 25-year-old Frank Jeffery arriving in 1952 as the school's first dedicated biologist. The then headmaster Garnons-Williams, suggesting that the subject be taught like the discipline itself, from little seeds that made up the first form gradually working the subject up with them as they rose through the school.

Having stayed put throughout the war – largely a pragmatic decision made so as not to lose numbers – Plymouth College came through the experience relatively unscathed. Furthermore, the fact that they had continued to play cricket and rugby at Ford Park, provided some cheer for those sports fans deprived of action through the wartime suspension of activities at Argyle, Albion, and Plymouth Cricket Club.

In the post-war period the school continued to prosper with a new man at the helm, Basil Garnons-Williams, his predecessor, Herbert Ralph having retired in 1945. Ralph had arrived at Ford Park back in the late-1920s and celebrated his 60th birthday just a week or two after VE Day. He had stayed on primarily to steer the school through those dark days of war: it had been a good decision.

While most of the evacuated local schools had settled back to some sort of normality before the end of the war, Mount House, the independent prep school that had been based at Hartley before evacuating to Tavistock, never returned. Requisitioned by the Admiralty shortly after it had been evacuated, Plymouth College made ready to move its Preparatory section into the Mount House site in 1946, although in the event the move didn't take place until the following year.

That same year, coincidentally, saw the reintroduction of National Service. First introduced during the war, it was stopped in 1945 only to be reintroduced, for males only, in 1947, essentially to swell the ranks of the armed forces.

Initially introduced for an 18-month term, it was later increased to two years and the scheme ran throughout the 1950s.

Left, Top and Bottom: The Plymouth College gymnasium sees service as an examination room, physical excercise space, orchestra rehearsal room and stage. Opposite page clockwise: Plymouth College 1st XV; outdoor swimming-pool, school magazine cover; aerial view of the school; cricket XI, and sports day.

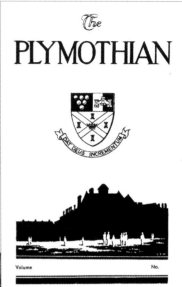

The
PLYMOTHIAN

DAT DEUS INCREMENTUM

Volume   No.

With a cadet corps tradition that stretched back to the nineteenth century, Plymouth College boys were well-placed to feed into this compulsory scheme, although it did mean that they lost more old boys during the two World Wars than other local schools.

Inspection Day was ever a feature at Ford Park, the Combined Cadet Force parading lads from all three sections – Army, Navy and Air Force – with the Army invariably the largest of the three and the RAF the smallest. Notwithstanding the numbers involved in any of the sections, most lads were more interested in Field Days and the Annual Camps than they were in standing still for hours on the school playing field, waiting for the arrival of the visiting inspector, or in marching around the perimeter of the school site. For the school generally, Speech Day was the showpiece event for both pupils and parents and like a number of other schools locally, with the enforced absence of the blitzed Guildhall, Central Methodist Hall was pressed into service for such occasions. It was also used by the City Council who were without both the Guildhall and the Municipal Building.

Top: *Annual Inspection of the Plymouth College Combined Cadet Force, 31 May 1954, Brigadeer Creedon takes the salute.* Bottom left: *Cadets march around a relatively deserted Devon Terrace, Brigadeer Bramwell David is the inspecting officer.* Bottom right: *Winners of the School inter-House Small Bore .22 Shooting Competition, 1954 with Messrs Canniford, Turpitt and Macnamara in the front row.*

Central Methodist Hall, Main School Speech Day, 1951, with Basil Garnons Williams, Headmaster, seated in the middle.

1951 Festival of Britain Jamboree at Mount Edgcumbe

Still with young people in uniform, the cub and scout movement prospered in the post-war period. The Plymouth Scouts in particular were singled out for praise by Chief Scout Lord Rowallan when addressing the first major local scouting event after the war at Mount Edgcumbe in the summer of 1946. The former Commander-in-Chief of Plymouth, Admiral Sir Ralph Leatham had previously appraised the Chief-Scout of the fine work done by local scouts during the war years.

Some 2,000 cubs and scouts attended that Jamboree, with a similar number turning out six years later, over the weekend of 6-8 July, when the movement again selected Mount Edgcumbe as their venue. Chief Executive Commissioner AW Hurll was the principal guest on this occasion, Scott of the Antarctic was the theme and the Jamboree was blessed with almost ideal weather.

In 1954 however, the Devon Jamboree was held in Torquay, while the local Gang Show that year was staged at the then new Honicknowle Secondary Modern School.

The headquarters of the Plymouth & District Boy Scouts' Association was, at this time, based in Buckland House, in Buckland Street, between the Continental Hotel and Union Street.

Above: *Graham Brooks entertains fellow scouts, 1953*

Top and Bottom: *Further scenes from the 1951 Festival of Britain Jamboree at Mount Edgcumbe.*

The Scouting Movement of course was by no means an exclusively male domain and there was no shortage of Brownies, Guides and Sea Rangers (a senior section of the Girl Guides and counterparts of the Sea Scouts) who were kitted out in white blouses, navy skirts, scarf, woggle and lanyard, all topped off with a matelot's hat. There were two companies in Plymouth, one linked to the SRS Devonshire, the others from St Peter's and Central District, to SS Muskateer.

As well as taking part in the major Jamborees, the girls too did their fair share of marching around town and performing in the fair sex equivalent of the Gang Show.

And then there was the Girls' Brigade, the female version of the Boys' Brigade, an organisation with an even longer history than Baden Powell's Scouting organisation.

Instituted nationally by William Smith, a serving officer with the 1st Lanarkshire Rifle Volunteers and a Sunday school teacher to boot, the first company was formed in Glasgow in 1883 and within four years had spread all over Scotland, into England and as far south as Plymouth. By the end of the nineteenth century there were more than a dozen companies across the Three Towns and after the Second World War yet more companies of this more militaristic outfit were formed, after many Boys' Brigade members had been helpful within the work of the Civil Defence set up during the war.

Top left: *Taking the salute from the then new Chief Scout, Lord Rowallan, at the Jamboree at Mount Edgcumbe, 20/21 July 1946* Bottom left and Above: *North Road Station, 31 July 1948, picture includes; Skipper Marjorie Cross, Anne Reckerby, Dessie Dawe, June Moore, Jean Shier, Aileen Ferris, Audrey Bevis, Susan Norton, Betty Chant, 'Willy' Williams, Sandy Sanderson and 'Matey'.*

Top left: *Marching down Royal Parade 1945/6 with Pamela Bond (centre front), Betty Millman, Patricia Twigg, Pamela Dodd, Dessie Dawe, Ann Rickaby, Jean Tucker and Eileen Watson.* Top right: *Marching through Union Street.* Bottom: *Girls' Brigade lead a Coronation March at Lipson Vale.*

Meanwhile, something that involved more of a trek than a march was the trip thousands of Plymouth school children made each year from Cremyll to Maker on the Rame Peninsula.

Taking the ferry from Admiral's Hard, Stonehouse, parties would arrive at Cremyll and head off for the heights of Maker where a regimented array of Nissen huts would be waiting to accommodate them: all set up for a week's worth of fun and games, with plenty of inter-school rivalry, swimming at Kingsand and Cawsand, and pillow fights after lights out.

These were happy days for a generation of young people half of whom would probably have had no other holiday away from home and half of those that did would not have stayed away overnight. So these Maker breaks were especially cherished, supervised by teachers, but away from parents. The youngsters were invariably encouraged to look after themselves as much as possible, particularly with regard to catering and cleaning.

Luckier still perhaps were those schoolchildren who went on overseas trips. With only around 2 per cent of the British population enjoying foreign holidays, a school trip to somewhere on the Continent opened an exciting window on another culture at a time when opportunities for such access were otherwise very limited.

Exchange trips were particularly popular, with many children getting a chance to visit pen-friends in places their parents had never been to – France, Germany, Italy – and indeed that was symptomatic of a bigger picture still – for as the raising of the school leaving age was keeping increasing numbers of young people within the school system, so the range of experiences open to those young people was increasing as well.

Hand in hand, with this somewhat slower entry into the real world, came a gradual relaxation of the rationing that had made for a relatively austere post-war environment. As the fifties progressed so the economy improved, allowing the emergence – and flowering – of this newly-created subsection of society – the teenager.

It took a while for anyone to notice, but once the market place cottoned on to the fact that there was a significant body of people out there that weren't yet classified as adults, but had grown out of most things childish – clothing, toys and entertainment – then changes were inevitable. The real revolution came with the advent of rock and roll in the middle of the fifties, but the signs were already there before that.

Top Left: Maker Camp group, back row; Elizabeth Brooks, Joyce Higgs, Miss Tilden, Joan Michel, Susan Lawrence. Front row: Rosylan Leverson, Joyce Pearce, Christine Brock and Judith Burt. Middle: The Camp site. Bottom: Moorfield School foreign trip 1955.

Clockwise from top left: *DHS for Girls 2nd XI hockey, 1952; Fifteen-year-old Valerie Catterall (third from left) wins the PPSA, Port of Plymouth, John Cocks Cup.; Hill Lane tennis players with Angela Mortimer c1951; Trophy time at Hill Lane, 1952.*

It can have been no real coincidence that in the same year as the School Leaving Age was raised, 1944, the National Association of Girls' Clubs, which had been founded just before the Great War, was re-branded the National Association of Girls' Clubs and Mixed Clubs (contracted to the National Association of Youth Clubs in 1961).

Soft drinks, sweets, table tennis, snooker and a record player were key elements in the setting up of such clubs, with church halls the usual venue. In the absence of any purely popular music radio station the arrival of the 45 rpm single did much to transform the atmosphere and popularity of the youth club, as well as confer some sort of defining identity.

Small wonder that the Pop Charts, or Hit Parade in this country was launched in 1952, along with all the new comics, books and toys with wide-ranging appeal, like Airfix kits (the first model, in 1949, was a tractor, then in 1954 a kit was produced of Drake's Golden Hind, with the first airplane, a Spitfire, in 1955). Lesney's (named after co-founders Leslie and Rodney Smith) Matchbox toys were another product of the early fifties, director Jack Odell making the breakthrough in response to a rule at his daughter's school which forbade the taking into school of any toy that couldn't fit in a matchbox (interestingly enough in the post-war climate of rebuilding Britain the first three Matchbox models were a green and red road roller, a dump truck and a cement mixer).

Dinky Toys, small although not as dinky or as small as Matchbox models, but around since the thirties (part of the Meccano and Hornby empire), started boxing their models around the same time.

High Street Secondary Modern School football team – 1950.

Top: *Sutton High School Athletic Team 1951: AC White, CL Oram, MD Randall, BW Edwards, GT Curnow, GB Firth, LE Abbott, NJ Steer, DE Dymond; front row: Dr CF Jones, AN Ward, WJ Phipps, CF Simpson, TN Cole, RH Chappell, Mr SJ Ebsary and WL Rendle. Bottom: Plympton Grammar School hockey team; Harry Grey, Pop Worthy, Syd Dymond, Kakus Roberts, Roger Ferris, Bouncer Hill. Front; Mudge, Hannam, Phil Duncan, Cyril Sherrell, Alex Johnson.*

Prince Rock U13 team 1949: l-r; Dave Potter, Bob Barnes, Bobby Burns, Dave Manley, Michael Prowse, Norman Martin, Brian Leman (with the trophy), David Hurrell, Victor Furneaux, Dave Rendle and Bill Dunn.

Playing with toy diggers and dump-trucks, and model trains and planes was one thing, but tinkering with bikes and adapting them for rallies and races was another challenge altogether and in open imitation of the motorized sport, cycle speedway was not only popular with the would-be big boys, it was also, in those pre-tv days, popular with friends and neighbours too. It wasn't unknown for crowds of 500 to turn out from time to time to watch the Ford Phantoms flying around their cinder track – the Marsh – towards the bottom of St Levan Road, battling it out with one of the other teams in the local league. On an evening like that it was often possible to pull in as much as £50 towards running costs – which included paying 7/6d (37p) to the league referee (who was also likely to put in a claim for his bus fare too).

'The oval track was marked out with old wartime fire hoses which had been whitewashed and nailed into place. None of our equipment was bought in – it was all cobbled together by someone keen to help out. The starting-gate was fairly rudimentary – three elastic lengths fixed to a pole and stretched across the width of the track, held with a long pin to a pole (usually a bit of five-by-four) on the other side. If you were too quick off the mark you ran the risk of losing a few spokes as the eyelets on the end of the elastic whipped across the track.' Roger Williamson.

Meanwhile, the starting-gates on the Traders Field track at Colebrook, off Newnham Road, were made for the team by Frank Harris the local blacksmith, while Bert Francis, the coal supplier to the village, used his lorry to transport the team, and their bicycles, to away matches.

Dedicated riders saved up all their pocket money and would regularly visit one or other of the local cycle shops (Battery Cycle Works, Embankment Road, Argyle Cycle Store, Stoke, the Cycle Shop, Fore Street, Torpoint) and buy something to help refine their machines ... one piece at a time.

Top: Laira Wasps v Foulston Eagles at St Budeaux - 1948 with Cyril Chapman (Wasps) and Arthur Chapman (Eagles). Bottom: Blockhouse, Stoke; Cecil Watkins in the middle and Penfold of Stoke and Parker of the Aces are on the inside.

Top left: *Terry Passmore collects the Mascot Cycle Speedway Championship trophy, with Roger Williamson second from right with his Green Ace of Clubs tabard.* Top right: *St Levan's Road, Ford, Cecil in civvies in the middle again.* Bottom right: *Dean Cross – Plymstock Lions v Foulston Eagles with Gerald Gould leading the field.* Bottom left: *Ernesettle Boars.*

Typically, teams were run on a shoestring too, although as the sport gained ground some of the more successful sides adopted more professional practices.

'With the Foulston Eagles you didn't ride your own bike, they were all held and looked after by Hoskin the mechanic, once he had your bike you didn't get it back. We didn't even have to pay for any of the transport costs on our away journeys and we even had an allowance for food and ice-creams.' Cecil Watkins.

Like their local heroes, the Plymouth Devils' Speedway team, the cycle speedway enthusiasts all had their own tabards and nicknames, the latter generally inspiring the motif on the former.

Ford Phantoms, for example, had a white ghost on a royal blue background. Meanwhile, other teams locally included the Stoke Dragons, State Millers, Plympton Monarchs, Plymstock Lions, Colebrook Tigers, Yealmpton Badgers, Foulston Eagles, Ernesettle Boars, Honicknowle Hornets, Laira Wasps and Torpoint Flyers.

Above: At the home of the State Devils, St Budeaux (State Cinema to the left), back row includes; team chairman Miles, Mr Curtain, Fred Millington secretary, P Mitchell, Horsham, Alan Dabnett, manager Osborne in the flat cap behind him, W Hoskin the mechanic and four others. Front row; D Blackmore, Cecil Watkins and H Hallet.
Middle 1: 1952 Stoke Dragons: L-R; Arthur Lavis, Colin Cotton, Brian Charlick, Bill Hutchings, Bill Gilbert, Ray Wood, Manager Ginger Hammett, Dave Oats. Front, mascot, ten-year-old Terry Passmore. 2: The Ford Phantoms c1953 includes; Maurice Hyde, Elliott, Garrett. Front; Cowell, Roger Williamson, Skinner, Clark. 3: Toproint Flyers. 4: 1952 Stoke Dragons v Plymstock Lions at the Blockhouse – note the crowd. Colin Cotton left, John Sylvester right (in white caps). Far right: various club badges.

Action at Pennycross Stadium.

SPORTING LIFE

There had been no Speedway at Pennycross during the war years, but it wasn't necessarily on account of the war that that situation had come to pass, as the sport, locally, had spluttered to a stop two years before war had been declared.

There had been one meeting in 1937 when an England side had ridden against an Australian team with a number of former local riders taking part. A crowd of just under 5,000 turned out for the event – about half the pre-war peak for the sport which had been introduced to the City in 1929.

Originally competing in the National League as the Plymouth Tigers, they had enjoyed one reasonably good season in 1933, but struggled in 1934 and promoters Western Speedway Ltd announced they would not be continuing their interest: it looked like Speedway at Pennycross was going to falter then, however a new promoter, Jack Colebach, picked it up.

Retaining the now familiar orange and white livery, Colebach restyled the team the Plymouth Panthers (these earlier names prompting the cycle speedway Tigers, Lions etc.), but still they struggled and enthusiasm for the sport waned.

The post-war revival came in 1947.

Unlike Home Park, Pennycross had been spared major damage during the war and as part of the revival process Plymouth's speedway team was rechristened 'the Devils' their new logo becoming a red devil set on a yellow background: and the man who ushered in these changes was the man who had introduced the sport to Plymouth in the first place – George 'Jimmy' Baxter.

Above: The Plymouth Speedway team of 1954: back l-r; Cyril Gray (promoter), Jackie Gates, Alan Smith, Don Weekes (team manager), George Wall (captain), Bill Thatcher, Kevin Hayden, Freddie Frape (track manager). Front; Harold Bull, Kevin Bock, Hec Mayhead, Ken Holmes, Pete Lansdale.

Baxter had, by this stage, promoted speedway all around the country - Glasgow, London and Southampton, as well as Plymouth - and now he became 'Director of Racing' at Pennycross. Operating under the aegis of Southern Speedways Limited, which also ran the speedway at Southampton, the Saints and the Devils (the nickname clearly apt in the event of south coast rivalry) were entered into the new Third Division of the National League.

The Saints were considerably the better of the two however, losing out on becoming league champions by just one point that season. The Devils, on the other hand, finished nine points adrift at the bottom of the table. Nevertheless there was undoubtedly an appetite for the sport and crowds consistently topped the 10,000 mark, and as the season ended with a reasonably stable squad of riders, there was a degree of optimism in the air.

The 1948 season opened with a meeting attended by an all-time record crowd of some 20,000 speedway fans and with Peter Robinson and Pete Lansdale signing from Southampton, forming a formidable heat-leading trio with former Norwich rider Len Read, hopes for the coming season were high (something Read never was: very slight and only 5'0" he added weights under his saddle for stability – nevertheless he become a giant of the sport, acquiring the epithet of the 'Mighty Atom').

Alex Gray, Bonnie Waddell, Vic Gent and Ivan Kessell were among the other Pennycross favourites (Kessell, incidentally, was a lay preacher, hence a committed Christian and he loathed wearing the club's Devils tabard and abandoned his jacket whenever he could). Notwithstanding the extra talent on offer, the Devils didn't overly distinguish themselves that season, however they did secure an important victory over Exeter, the eventual champions, at the end of August.

'That victory helped to make up for the big 65-31 defeat at Exeter on 24 May when sugar was found in the fuel tanks of Plymouth riders Lansdale and Robinson.' (Paul Eustace - *Plymouth Speedway*)

Lansdale, Robinson and Read spearheaded the 1949 campaign, on a home track that now used powdered brick dust where there had previously been crushed granite from the Moors. Lansdale had a great season for the club, and finished joint top scorer in the Third Division with the feted Billy Bales of Yarmouth.

'Bales made a huge impression at Pennycross in June when he knocked two full seconds off the track record. The Plymouth officials demanded that his engine should be checked. This was done and the motor declared perfectly legal.' (Lethbridge: *Speedway in the South West*)

Top and Bottom: *Action from Pennycross.* Top: *11 June 1949 Len Read (Plymouth) leads Ron Howes (Rayleigh), Alan Smith (P) and Charlie Mugford (R)*

Above: *Plymouth Devils fans, c.1950, with Marjorie Southard.* Inset: *Trelawney's Coronation Queen, Jean Edwards with George Wall and Bill Thatcher at Pennycross Stadium, 1953.*

It had been Plymouth's best ever season, they had finished third and were promoted as the Second Division was expanded from 12 to 15 teams.

Although their away form was lacking, the Devils enjoyed a flying start to their first season in the new league, winning their first eight home matches. Then came Glasgow who inflicted the first of three home defeats on the Plymouth club, the others being at the hands of Edinburgh and Cradley Heath – the Heathens.

The Heathens had only been founded a few years earlier (in 1947) but were a strong side - they finished third that season, but were thumped 56-28 by the Devils when they visited the West Midlands that July.

In the event the Devils finished ninth and with six teams below them should have been safe, particularly as the league was expanded further for the coming season, however a number of the more northerly promoters didn't like Plymouth's 'geographical location' and conspired successfully to have the Devils demoted.

It was a bitter pill and one that was made even worse by the departure of their main stars. Walthamstow snapped up Pete Lansdale, while Liverpool secured the services of both Peter Robinson and Len Read.

What made matters worse was that Liverpool hadn't exactly set the Third Division on fire and the man who master-minded Robinson and Read's move was promoter Jimmy Baxter. Baxter also recruited a couple of Southampton's stars for the Liverpool Chads.

Many fans voted with their feet and attendances at Pennycross dwindled; meanwhile, Southampton were unable to fulfil their Second Division fixture list and folded after only seven matches.

Freddie Parr came in as the new promoter in Plymouth, while the former Exeter and Poole rider, Sid Hazzard, became the new team manager.

In an attempt to win back the crowds, Hazzard introduced a couple of new events, side-car racing and midget-car racing. For the latter he engaged the services of one of the Plymouth-based junior riders, Brian Hitchcock, who was a fitter in the dockyard. Working together the two of them built several midget racing cars and staged special meetings to showcase them.

Overall the season was unremarkable however, but with the return of Pete Lansdale, the level of anticipation surrounding the 1952 in what was now the Southern League – as opposed to Division Three - was much higher.

Autumn 1952 and a new sport arrives in the city - midget racing. Top right: Speedway rider and dockyard fitter, Brian Hitchcock in a 500cc Arnott on a snowy Pennycross Stadium track. The first meeting on 14 November attracted a crowd of over 11,000 and featured 1000cc four-wheel drive machines, but the sport didn't really catch on. Above: A 1952 midget racer.

With George Wall and Alan Smith adding strength to Lansdale and Bill Kitchen (back from injury) the team enjoyed a run of success, but then Hazzard left and Lansdale left again and the team finished up a respectable third in the league. The highlight of the season for many local speedway fans came when England 'C' rode out against a Swedish side in front of almost 10,000.

In 1953 Lansdale, who had retired early the previous season, made another comeback, and Len Read also made a welcome return to Pennycross. It was a season marred by accidents: skipper Goerge Wall was injured in a pre-season incident, which later forced him to retire on medical grounds; Bill Thatcher suffered a fractured skull at Southampton, but more tragically 23-year-old Australian rider Ted Stevens was fatally injured at St Austell on 14 April 1953.

'Ken Monk, of St Austell, was leading team-mate Jackie Gates, when he over-slid on a bend. Stevens who was immediately behind the Cornish pair, struck one of the other rider's machines and was flung into the safety fence. He died before reaching hospital. Monk fractured his collarbone and Gates (another Australian) injured his leg, but carried on racing.' (John Walters)

It was the second fatality the Devil's had suffered in two years, following the accident in May 1951 when 36-year-old Dick Jenkins, making his first appearance at Pennycross, raced down the back straight at full throttle and then failed to negotiate the bend and rode up over the fence on to the greyhound track on the other side.

However, the various problems experienced by the Plymouth team were by no means unique to the Pennycross outfit. The St Austell team folded at the end of the 1953 season and in yet another attempt to reinvigorate the sport the Second Division and the Southern League were amalgamated as National League Division Two at the start of the 1954 season.

Despite the presence of firm favourites Alan Smith, Pete Lansdale, Bill Thatcher and, riding against medical advice, George Wall, the sport locally was dogged by poor crowds and abysmal weather. An early exit from the National Trophy was followed by a couple of crushing blows in the Southern Shield. Attendances dropped, admission prices rose, but the numbers didn't stack up. Crowds of 4,500 were needed to break even, but the average figure was 1,000 less than that. Thursday 1 July was the date scheduled for their third league match of the season: but the rain came and the fixture was cancelled.

Above: Ted Stevens who died after an accident on the track on 14 April 1953. Left: 'Devonport Motor Cycle Club used to stage pillion trials on the Moors: standard bikes, ordinary clothes and a passenger - either a mate or a girlfriend - the idea was that riding on slippery ground would make us better riders' Sandy Pimlott.

In the event, there would be no more league speedway at Pennycross for five years. The last match there was a World Championship qualifier which took place the following Thursday – 8 July 1954. Conditions again were awful, the track was treacherous and the visibility poor, as a heavy misty drizzle filled the air. It was an inauspicious end to what had been a very popular diversion for thousands of local speedway fans.

However within a week a new sport arrived at the stadium – stock car racing - and this proved an instant hit, regularly attracting crowds twice the size of that following the two-wheeled entertainment.

'If midgets had whetted the appetite for oval-track car racing then the introduction of of stock car racing in 1954 provided the main course. It had arrived that year from America, via France and Belgium, and was promoted more like a circus than a sport. Big American cars, with big bumpers and plenty of contact, made for spectacular action.'
(Andrew Weltch *Oval Racing in Devon and Cornwall*)

A crowd of over 12,000 turned out for the first meeting on Thursday 15 July while the second meeting added another 3,000 to the gate.

Stock Car Racing filled the 7.45pm Thursday slot at Pennycross with Greyhound Racing ever popular on a Wednesday evening at 7.30pm.

Greyhound Racing had been popular in Britain since the late eighteenth century, but the sport really gained a hold in the early twentieth century when an American businessman devised a version of the sport that used artificial lures, rather than live ones. The idea was brought across the Atlantic by Charles Munn, who set up the Greyhound Racing Association Trust in 1925. It wasn't long before a track had been set up in Belle Vue, Manchester, and then, in 1927 the near-derelict White City Stadium in London was acquired and the GRA moved their headquarters to the capital.

That same year the Greyhound Racing Association (Plymouth) was constituted, one of eighteen locations targeted around the country.

Then, over the bank holiday Whit weekend of May 1928, the Stadium at Pennycross opened with four flat and three hurdle races. Admission charges ranged from 1/7d to 5/- (7p to 25p) with car parking available for one shilling. The vast majority of punters however accessed the stadium via bus or on foot as the sport became a huge hit with the working man.

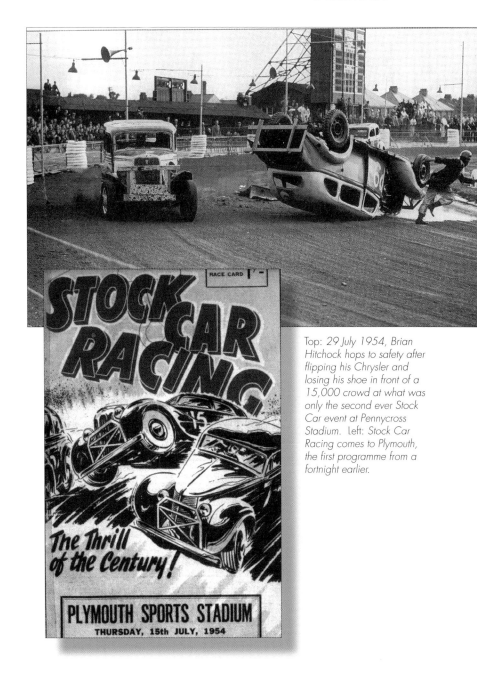

Top: *29 July 1954, Brian Hitchock hops to safety after flipping his Chrysler and losing his shoe in front of a 15,000 crowd at what was only the second ever Stock Car event at Pennycross Stadium.* Left: *Stock Car Racing comes to Plymouth, the first programme from a fortnight earlier.*

In no time at all millions of men were having a weekly flutter on the dogs and after the war the numbers continued to grow peaking with attendances of around 30 million a year across more than 40 tracks around the country, putting it almost on a par with football.

In addition to the obvious appeal of the gambling, greyhound racing offered the added attraction of a night out. Football was not yet a floodlit sport and so there was something special about the atmosphere surrounding this exciting evening activities here at Meanwhile, just a few hundred yards away at Beacon Park, one of the other more exciting outdoor events locally was wrestling.

Wrestling had had a bit of a bad press in the late thirties and initial attempts to relaunch the sport after the war struggled, however Admiral Lord Mountevans was a big fan of the sport and together with Commander AB Campbell (another distinguished naval figure and a member of the popular Brains Trust radio panel show), MP Maurice Webb and Olympic Wrestler Norman Morell, he assembled a committee to produce an official set of rules for the sport.

Locally, Les Eastlick, a former Devonport Boxing Club protege who fought under the somewhat more exotic ring-name of Elmo Marcelle, had introduced wrestling to the area just before the war, not long after switching to the discipline himself. After the hostilities had ceased, Les, still appearing under the Elmo guise, re-invented himself as a boxing and wrestling ref after he'd been demobbed in 1947 (he'd served as a PTI, Physical Training Instructor, during the war). Armed now with a set of rules for across seven different weight divisions, he refereed thousands of bouts and was regularly in the ring at Beacon Park trying to maintain order.

Complementing the facilities at Pennycross and Beacon Park were the sports grounds and buildings of the Civil Service Club off the aptly named Recreation Road. Boasting an opening post-war membership of 5,000, all the popular sports sides were up and running by 1946, and by June 1948, when the club's 21st birthday celebrations were held at Beacon Down, there was across-the-board action from the cricket, tennis, table tennis, bowls, billiards, snooker and darts sections. In addition to which there was also an athletics competition, with a full range of sprints, plus a mile and a three-mile race.

There were also football and rugby teams as well as a motoring section and other minority sports.

Elmo Marcelle (aka Les Eastlick) refereeing wrestling bouts at Beacon Park c.1950

Inset: *The new clubhouse, completed in 1949.* Above: *A game of bowls played in 1948 as part of the 21ist Anniversary celebrations.*

Schoolboy coxswain Fernley Tranter collects a trophy on behalf of the Morice Town rowers circa 1946

Of course, one of the most prestigious sporting clubs in the city was the Royal Western Yacht Club: their pre-war premises, alongside the Grand Hotel on the Hoe, had taken a direct hit on Monday 21 April 1941 and the front of the club had been destroyed and a number of bedrooms wrecked. Plans were then made to remove as much as possible from the club to an underground location in the Citadel. A couple of lorries were booked for the Wednesday, but fate intervened and on Tuesday night further enemy action destroyed all that was left.

A letter sent from Windsor Castle to Lord Mount Edgcumbe acknowledged that the King, who was the Club's Patron, 'was very sorry to hear of the destruction of the Royal Western Yacht Club of England.'

A temporary home was found in Leigham Street, before premises were offered in No.6 The Esplanade. The following year No.5 was purchased for £1,650 by the Club's Honorary Secretary and the club agreed to rent the premises from him. In 1943 a Billiard Room was opened in the building and the following year the Club agreed to exercise an option to purchase No.5 from Mr Andrew at that same price. In the event, eight years later the Club accepted a *'very satisfactory settlement ... free of all costs, in respect of war damage to the old Club House of £30,000'*.

They then looked at the possibility of purchasing the properties either side of No.5 but neither owner was prepared to sell.

The Royal Western, although they had lost a great deal, were now nicely positioned and over the next few years there was talk of amalgamation with the two other Royal yacht clubs in the city.

In the meantime various races were organised, and 'finished' by the Club, including a Transatlantic Race in 1952 and the Fastnet Race in 1953.

There were also several other clubs of consequence in the area, among them: the Royal South Western, the Royal Plymouth Corinthian, Mayflower Sailing Club, Sutton Harbour, West Hoe and the Royal Naval Sailing Association.

There were also a number of local rowing clubs too, and competition between them could be fierce. Among the most keenly contested was that played out between the Morice Town Rowers and the local Naval teams – and it was not unknown for quite large sums of money to change hands over the outcome.

Top: *1953 Commander-in-Chief's Cup Race for Service dinghies in Plymouth Sound.*
Left: *18 May 1952, 39-year-old Mrs Ann Davison leaving Plymouth in the Cremyll-built 'Felicity Ann' attempting to become the first woman to cross the Atlantic single-handed. On 23 January 1953 she eventually made it and would later chronicle her story in the book My Ship Is So Small.*

Opened at the end of the summer of 1938, the new pavilion at Peverell Park only saw one full season of use before the war intervened and over the next eight years the fine art-deco building was thrown into service as a school annex, with pupils from Hyde Park being the most regular 'tenants'.

Even after the war the pavilion was still being used Monday to Friday as a school and it wasn't until 1947 that Plymouth Cricket Club eventually managed to get back into their building properly.

Of those who came together to relaunch the club that year only a handful had been part of the Plymouth set up before the war – four from the 1st XI but no-one from the 2nds. Nevertheless, within a couple of months there were over 40 playing members on the club's books; there were new nets, and seating for over 300 (most of it purchased from the now redundant air raid shelters).

Thirty-five-year-old Ernie Carless (the former Glamorgan wicket keeper, who could also bat and bowl, and who had played football professionally for Cardiff City before the war) was brought in as club professional, while a true old-stager, Sid Solomon (who had first played for Plymouth in 1902) made something of a comeback. He clearly had plenty still to offer, having once claimed the wicket of WG Grace. Sid returned figures of 7-23 as Plymouth skittled out Plymouth College for 61 in June 1947.

The first day of May 1948 marked the official rebirth of the club, Lord Mayor Herbert Perry officiating and noting that the club deserved better recognition by the County Board. However, the club's main gripes were aimed at the Local Authority itself, the principal complaint being that their rates bill (£150 per annum) was two and half times that of Torquay CC, and that, together with a ground rent of £40 per year, made things very tight.

The situation would undoubtedly have been easier if they had been able to charge for admission, but with access possible around almost any part of the boundary that was hopeless, so that they had to rely on passing a tin around the spectators.

As it was numbers varied enormously: around 600 turned out for a game against United Services and the annual encounter with Plymouth Argyle always drew a decent crowd. However, as the fifties progressed there was ever more competition from other areas, and on Saturday 5 May 1956 only 17/6d was collected in gate money, the big rival attraction being the televised FA Cup final between Manchester City and Birmingham City.

Plymouth Cricket Club at Peverell Park

South Devon players look on as their skipper, Francis Cundy anticipates the toss at Peverell. Len Coldwell, collar upturned, who went on to play for Worcester and England is third from the right.

SOUTH WESTERN COUNTIES
(CORNWALL, DEVON, DORSET & WILTS)
RUGBY UNION

SOUTH AFRICA
(SPRINGBOKS)

HOME PARK
PLYMOUTH

SATURDAY, 13th OCTOBER, 1951
KICK-OFF 3.15 p.m.

BAND OF H.M. ROYAL MARINES (PLYMOUTH)
by permission of Colonel K. L. M. COOPER, O.B.E.
Director of Music: Captain R. H. STONER, L.R.A.M.
(in co-operation with the National Savings Committee)

WE EXTEND A REAL WESTCOUNTRY WELCOME
TO OUR VISITORS FROM THE DOMINIONS

★

Official Programme 3d.

Rugby at Home Park: Saturday 13 October 1951 (Argyle were away at Northampton); Peter Luffman (Albion), BA Viviers (Springboks), John 'Ginger' Williams (Penzance-Newlyn), John Collins (Camborne), F Marais (SA) and Lieut RM Holgate (Devonport Services).

While football may have affected the numbers supporting cricket from time to time, those interested in egg chasing were generally less fickle. Certainly there were a number of highlights in those immediate post war years, not least of which was the visit of the South African rugby team to Home Park on Saturday 13 October 1951.

The opposition was an amalgam of local clubs – a South West Counties side – including Peter Luffman from Albion and Lieutenant RM Holgate and BM Gray from Devonport Services. Argyle were away at Northampton that weekend, they lost 3-1 as it happened, Jumbo Chisholm scoring the Pilgrims only goal (it was also the only goal he scored that season).

The Springboks had a very strong touring party, their game against the South West Counties was only their second game of what would end up being a total of 31 matches, 30 of which they would go on to win, including the test series against the five home nations, England, Scotland, Wales, Ireland and France. In that context the fact that the South West Counties only lost 8-17 to Basil Kenyon's tourists says much about the strength of the local sides.

It should be remembered though that, at that time, a try was worth just three points – five if converted – and the value of a dropped goal had just been reduced from four to three points (in 1948).

Locally Plymouth Albion, with George Wakeham of Carkeeks as a principal sponsor, tended to have the strongest fixture list but Devonport Services sometimes had the star players – largely thanks to the availability of quality young rugby lads doing National Service. Several Services players, in those early post-war years, were selected to represent their country, among them eight who played for the Royal Navy against New Zealand in December 1945: WD Maclennan wing three-quarter (Scotland 1947), Les Williams, centre, and Grif Bevan, hooker (Wales 1947-48), MR Neely, front-row forward (Ireland 1947), WKT Moore, scrum half, JRC Matthews and DB Vaughan (England 1947-48-49). Lewis Jones, and Malcolm Thomas also played for Wales in the early fifties, along with one of England's leading forwards, D'Arcy Hoskin, the last three, along with Vaughan, playing in the same game at Twickenham, Saturday 21 January 1950 when England entertained Wales. The real highlight of that season for Services fans however was the re-opening of the Rectory. Most of the grandstand had been severely damaged during the Blitz, such that there was only enough space to accommodate about 50

Top: *Devonport Services c.1948.* Bottom: *Albion 1st XV 1953/4. Back row: Claude Harris (trainer), Bill Brooks, Bill Pellow, John Pascoe, Ray Ellis, Harold Biddle, Roy Ruston, Geoff Martin, Gordon Crimp, Wilf Nash (treas), Middle Row: Art Brokenshire (match sec), George Jeffrey, WHJ Priest, David Luffman, Les Semmens (capt), Rex Wiltshire, Roy Harris, Peter Luffman, Leighton Williams. Front Row: Frank Pocock, Peter Weevil, Eddie Hall, Bob Stephens*

Alf Woods jumps for a ball in a line-out, in a game between Albion and Cambourne.

supporters and it was decided that rather than attempt its repair it would be better to rebuild it entirely.

However, it wasn't quite that simple: a licence was required for any new building just as it was in any other part of the City, and with the severe shortage of housing in the area it was decided by the Committee that it would be morally wrong to apply for such a licence and thereby deprive the housing authorities of much needed building materials. And so it was that the most damaged part of the stand was stripped of anything useful and the salvaged materials used to patch up where possible and thereby provide accommodation for about 1,200.

At the same time it was proposed that when the building situation eased that a second stand would be erected on the other side of the pitch. The new facility would be known as the Luddington Memorial Stand, in honour of the late Bill Luddington who had lost his life in the war, and who had achieved the rare, if not unique distinction of being the only Naval Rating ever to have captained a Royal Navy XV.

There was plenty of support, official, financial, and practical – local Marines being called in to blast their way into areas of rock and shale that was making life difficult for the workmen.

Eventually, however, on 3 April 1950 the work was completed. A great supporter of the scheme, the former Commander-in-Chief, Sir Robert Burnett, was on hand to officiate and he in turn thanked everyone who had helped from Lord Nuffield, through the Sports Control Board, the RN Barracks Canteen Fund and the men of the 'lower deck' who had largely funded the terracing of the Luddington Stand on the popular side of the Rectory.

Interestingly enough, an analysis of the make-up of Devonport Services sides around this time showed that 134 players represented the club in one season (1953/54) of whom just over half were men from the 'lower deck' and a little under a third were officers (24 Royal Navy, 10 Army and 6 Royal Marines). Between them the 1st XV and 2nd XV managed 72 fixtures, just over half of which, 38, were won.

Other prominent 'junior' sides included Plymouth Argaum, with their own clubhouse in the north of the city, sponsored by landowner Tom HItchins, who had kick started their post-war revival with a meeting at the Lockyer Hotel, presided over by Leslie Paul and OPMs, OPO's and DHSOBs.

Top: *Argaum 1st XV, 1953-54.* Inset: *Tom Hitchins.* Bottom: *OPM RFC, awarded the RNE College Cup, 1953: Back row: B Mahoney, RJ Williams, K Pring, J Quick, J Lethbridge, R Southern, D Smale, J Beamish. Third row: G Tucker, R Pashley, C May, G Pengelly, R Stafford, J Hamley, A Goodenough, L King, J Reid. Second row: A Harvey, A Squire, J Northcott, R Pratt, T Mutton, P Vittle, N Elliott, N Blackler. Front: P Luddington and R Stott.*

Beacon Castle AFC 1947/48 with George Harper, his brother-in-law Fred Maher and nephew, Fred Maher jnr.

While a number of the local rugby teams relied heavily on the Services or the old boy network, the local football set up was generally based much more around the work place or the church or youth club. But not exclusively so: Stonehouse United were formed in 1950 by a group of ex-National Service boys. They bought their first set of kit from Millets in York Street: '£10 for a full set of Army surplus stuff – green and white shirts, white shorts, green stockings and two footballs. We had a badge for our blazers, taken from the Stonehouse crest – green and white squares with the heads of two boars.' (Dave Bromage)

Everything was done on a shoe-string with the team sponsoring themselves by selling raffle tickets and game cards. Most teams relied heavily on volunteers: someone to wash the kit, iron it, embroider badges or logos on to shirts and make sure the bladder in the heavy-duty leather ball was fully inflated and that the oranges were ready for half time.

Stonehouse United eventually made it into the Plymouth Combination League, and, having won that and the Combination Cup, the Plymouth & District Premier League. Some teams achieved interesting distinctions: Weston Mill Oak Villa (the name was taken from a cottage at Camel's Head where their first meeting had been held back in 1912) served as a nursery club for Brighton and Hove Albion in the early fifties – the club enjoyed a regular fixture against them over the Easter weekend at Millbay Park.

The Oak Villa first team travelled all over Devon and Cornwall playing teams like Totnes, Dartmouth, Torquay, Holsworthy, Millbrook and Torpoint, while the second team had an altogether more parochial set of fixtures: Gas Board, Pearn Brothers, Woodland Fort, Plymstock and the Green Waves.

Curiously enough, in the 1950/51 season, in the very early stages of FA Cup, Green Waves knocked out another local side – Plymouth United. United had competed twice before, in 1946 and 1947, losing both times to Dartmouth. Following their win Green Waves were knocked out in the next preliminary round by Truro City.

A couple of players, including Bill Adams and Jack Smith, of Plymouth United went on to join Argyle, the former in 1945 (he only played one game), the latter in late-1950 – later still, Jack went on to play several seasons at Torquay.

Frank Arundel and Reg Wyatt both graduated from Oak Villa to play for Argyle, George Wright, meanwhile, who was one of the few Argyle players to play for the club before and after the war, was a former Kitto Institute boy (he later became a favourite at Colchester), while Pat Jones and Reg Wyatt were both former Astor Institute lads. Both destined to become firm favourites at Home Park, Pat signing up in 1947 and going on to play 425 games for the club, Reg in 1950, playing over 200 games before moving on to Torquay some fourteen years later - the two played many games together.

Top: Stanbury United 1946 with trainer Charlie Simmons far left. Middle: Mount Gould Athletic includes Len Sullivan, Ivor Nicholls, Ken Jasper, Jack Edwards, Len Burns, Max Crook, Terry Peree, Harold Barnes. Bottom: West Down United.

10 January 1948. FA Cup 3rd rd. Argyle v Luton, 36,195 pile into Home Park to see Argyle lose 4-2. Note the spaces in the car park.

HOME PARK

Home Park had been commandeered during the war as a repository for furniture salvaged from houses that had been damaged in the pre-blitz raids on the city, thus it was little wonder, that when incendiaries did eventually rain down on the stadium there was little likelihood of preventing the conflagration. Everything – offices, dressing rooms, training quarters – was reduced to a shambles.

'The war had left the club with no money in the kitty and very little else but its name and reputation. Home Park itself was a picture of desolation with the grandstand reduced to a heap of rubble at the bottom of a huge crater, the grass had grown long and debris covered parts of that formerly well-kept playing pitch, and even the turnstiles had been removed to a place of safety and had to be located. Of the thirty-two players on the club's books in 1939, only ten were found to be available to return to Home Park when needed in 1945: no other club in the country had suffered more severely from the effects of the war.' (Sid Tonkin - All About Argyle 1963)

The football league programme had been suspended in just three games into the 1939/40 season, and although a South West Regional League was instituted to complete some sort of programme over the remainder of the season, there had been several fallow years.

2 October 1948 Argyle v Cardiff in front of 29,346 at Home Park (they lose 1-0)

147

Looks like they've both spotted the ball ... too late..

In 1944 an attempt to revive the game in area was made by the setting up of Plymouth City and Plymouth United, mainly with ex-Argyle and assorted local players, but it wasn't until the end of the war that any serious thought was given to the game nationally. Even then it was felt that it would be impractical to relaunch the league programme straight after the cessation of hostilities and so the top two leagues were divided on a north south basis and Argyle became part of the Football League (South). The club's unreadiness to compete was evidenced in a dismal set of results that saw them win just three games, one away (to Brentford), and two at home (to Nottingham Forest and Wolverhampton Wanderers, both times by a 3-2 margin). Argyle were the league's whipping boys, they didn't manage one clean sheet at Home Park, only one side failed to put three or more goals past them and ten of the 21 other teams scored seven or more.

It was as well that there was no promotion or relegation from the league, as Argyle ended up with a negative goal difference of 81, six points adrift at the bottom of the table. The only good thing was that attendances across the league were good, with Arsenal, Spurs, Chelsea and West Ham among the London teams included and Birmingham, Villa, Wolves and West Brom marking the northern extremity of the league. Many of these teams had managed to keep some sort of fixtures going through the war, unlike the massively disadvantaged Argyle.

The most important thing though was that Argyle had re-engaged and oblivion had been avoided. But it hadn't been easy even then: during that first post-war season manager Jack Tresarden had fielded no less than 72 different players – *'many of them untried local amateurs or servicemen – called upon to assist as guest players. These team-raising troubles often forced Mr Tresarden to leave Plymouth for an "away" match with just three or four players and collect others at the visiting ground or on the way.'* (Tonkin)

Servicemen arrived from all parts of the country, while it wasn't unknown for Argyle's goalkeeper, Matt Middleton, who'd been with them before the war, to end his week as a coalminer in Derby on a Friday and travel to Plymouth overnight for a game on the Saturday. Happily however, the real post-war programme started the following season, and it picked up with exactly the same fixture list as that which had been abandoned in 1939.

Postwar Argyle action.

Planning the new stand at Home Park.

Over 25,000 turned out to see West Ham return to Home Park for the opening game of the season and, seven years on, Argyle reversed the 1-3 scoreline, with Bill Strauss and left winger Sid Rawlings scoring for the Greens. The latter, a signing from Everton, netted twice and would go on to score 17 goals that season, the same number as inside left Rob Thomas and two fewer than Rob's older brother, Dave who, like Rob only missed one game all season.

The season started promisingly enough with Argyle losing only 5 of their first 18 games, but then came a 6-1 thumping away at Birmingham and thereafter they lost 18 of the last 24 games (11 of the last 12) and were lucky to avoid the drop. Ironically, however, they scored more goals than each of the top four clubs, including Manchester City who won the league.

It was difficult to apportion blame however, and as the manager, Jack Tresarden, was keen to point out, there were a number of factors at play: *'much talk was made about the team's performances, but few people realised some of the contributory causes of the unimpressive showing. The acute housing shortage in Plymouth at the time was an almost insurmountable obstacle that had to be overcome before players could be induced to come to Home Park. A number of married players were permitted to live in their home towns until houses could be found for them, but they were never really welded into the team through being with the club only once a week, and then, often after a long and tiring train journey, and their form suffered accordingly.'*

Ominously the following season started with another 6-1 drubbing, this time in front of 52,000 at Newcastle: nevertheless 24,000 eternally optimistic Argyle fans turned out for the first home match of the season, against Birmingham City. Birmingham won 3-0, and Argyle were floundering. By the time Newcastle came to Home Park, on 20 December, Argyle had won only three of their first 21 games, consequently few of the 26,603 who turned out for the pre-Christmas encounter dared to hope that Argyle might beat the high-flying Geordies, 3-0, but they did and again it marked something of a turning point as the second half of the season saw Argyle lose only four more games and once again avoid relegation (interestingly enough both Birmingham and Newcastle were promoted).

By that time the heavily pressured club manager/secretary Jack Tresarden had resigned and been replaced by Home Park favourite, on and off the pitch, Jimmy Rae.

Top: Thousands of tons of rubble from the devastated city centre was brought up to Home Park to fill the bomb craters and create better banking. Middle and bottom: The new stand is completed.

151

Left: *Jimmy Rae.* Above: *Argyle attack the Devonport end c.1948*

Rae's elevation to the top job was complemented by the appointment of Bert Cole as club secretary, thereby relieving the manager of a significant area of responsibility. However, it also, unfortunately, came at a time when *'football success was measured by the size of a club's cheque book, for just then, there was much talk about the size of the Argyle bank overdraft.'* (Tonkin)

Over the next two seasons Argyle continued to struggle, and the board continued to bicker. At the end of the 1948/49 season they finished one point above relegated Nottingham Forest with a much worse goal difference, losing the last game of the season 5-0 to Spurs in front of nearly 24,000 at Home Park.

It was a portentous result as the 1949/50 fixture list pitted the Pilgrims against Spurs, twice in August home and away in the first four games of the season. Argyle lost both encounters and would go on to win just eight league games all season, ending up in a relegation place, while Spurs would only lose eight games and finish the season runaway champions of Division Two.

A spirited end to the season had seen them lose just one of their last six games, and they finished just two points below Queens Park Rangers, a bitter pill when they'd beaten Rangers away from home but lost at Home Park in March. If only they had won that game ...

It was undoubtedly one of those seasons and most of the loyal supporters felt their side had been very unlucky and apart from conceding twice to Spurs, Argyle managed to take at least one point from their travels to each of the other sides in the top six and managed to beat Sheffield Wednesday (who were promoted with Tottenham) 4-2 at Bramhall Lane.

Certainly, at a time when some clubs were experiencing falling attendances, the Home Park gates were healthy, only dropping below 20,000 five times, and each of those was marked by bad weather.

The season wasn't all gloom by any means, with the undoubted highlight coming in the 3rd round of the FA Cup when Argyle were drawn at home against current cup holders Wolverhampton Wanderers. Over 42,000 managed to squeeze themselves into Home Park, where the famous trophy was paraded around the ground before kick-off. Argyle had led Billy Wright's side for much of the game after Stan Williams had managed to push Frank Squires' parried shot past England keeper Bert Williams.

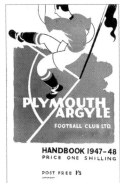
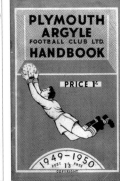

7 January 1950 Wolves bring the FA Cup to Home Park. Middle: Handbook cover 1947-8; 1948-9 and FA Cup 3rd rd. programme. Bottom: Supporters gather.

This page: *Torquay United pay tribute to Argyle as Division Three South champions, at the last home game of the season, 26 April 1952 - the game was drawn 2-2.*
Opposite page: *top: Argyle supporters on a trip north in the late 1940s.* Middle and bottom: *Local scenes greeting Argyle's promotion squad in 1952.*

However, a 70th minute equaliser dashed hopes of a victory and thousands of excited fans made plans for a trip to Molyneux four days later, on Wednesday 11 January.

Reading the programme notes, Argyle fans could be justifiably proud of their boys: *'When winning the FA Cup last season we had many hard fights, notably against Manchester United in the semi-final meeting, but even those drama-shrouded battles did not eclipse our meeting with Plymouth Argyle on Saturday. Here we would like to offer our sincere congratulations to the Second Division side on their really grand showing. For a club so low in the Second Division as to be faced with the prospect of relegation they played football of a surprisingly high quality and a maintenance of this must see them rise in the table.'*

In the event the replay turned out to be a much more one-sided affair with Argyle going down 3-0, but having performed so well against arguably the top side in the country (Wolves finished the season runners up in Division One, having won the League Championship three times since the war - they were knocked out of the Cup by Blackpool in a 5th round replay), they were all fired up for their next league match, that great away win against promotion chasing Sheffield Wednesday, with Billy Strauss, George Dews and Frank Squires all finding their way onto the score sheet.

Back in Division Three South, Argyle struggled initially, winning only three of their first ten matches, and scoring only eight goals – the tenth game being an ignominious 1-0 home defeat to arch rivals Exeter. Something then clicked and over the next eight games they found the net no less than 30 times, Tadman scoring most frequently, twice in the 7-1 rout of Colchester and four times in the 6-0 away win at Brighton. In the end they finished fourth, level on points with third-placed Reading. Crowds were down but regularly up around the 20,000 mark with the biggest gate of the season again coming in the FA Cup, when they were once more pitted against the mighty Wolves in the 3rd round. 40,000 filled Home Park once more and at half time the Third Division club were holding the visitors 1-1. Cruelly, however, a clash between players saw Pat Jones leaving the field for a vital 18 minutes (there were no substitutes). On his return the clearly concussed Jones was out of sorts and Argyle lost their shape with George Dews, Argyle's goalscorer dropping back to left back.

Argyle lost 2-1 and Wolves went on to the semi-finals, losing out to the winning finalists, Newcastle in a replay.

*Argyle line-up circa 1951. Back row: Johnny Porteous, Paddy Radcliffe, Pat Jones, Bill Shortt, Tony McShane, George Dews.
Front: Maurice Tadman, Neil Dougall, Jack Chisholm, Gordon Astall and Bill Strauss*

The following season 1951/52 Argyle started with a disappointing away defeat at Leyton Orient, but then won their next six consecutive matches and after another great run of eight wins on the trot, ultimately pipped Reading to finish top of the league with a tally of over 107 goals, Tadman (27) and Dews (25) scoring half of them, with Astall (18) and Rattray (19) adding greatly to the fire-power.

Back in Division Two Argyle had a flying start to the season and were unbeaten in their first seven games, including a memorable 5-2 home win against Sheffield United (the eventual league champions) in front of 30,000.

Tension mounted as Argyle looked as if they might get a second successive promotion and reach the top flight of English football for the first time in their history, however a lean spell either side of Christmas that yielded just one win in nine games, frustrated those ambitions and although they then put a five-win run together, they would ultimately finish fourth.

It wasn't the only disappointment that season: after consecutive home wins in the 3rd round of the FA Cup against Coventry and Barnsley in the 4th, Argyle fans started to dream of Wembley, or at least an historic first quarter-final encounter, particularly after being drawn to play at Home Park again in the 5th round against Gateshead who were only in the Third Division North. Almost 30,000 fans poured into the ground, its capacity somewhat reduced since the completion of the new stand.

The atmosphere was electric, Argyle played some attractive football, Gateshead appeared to be holding out for a replay and played a spoiling game. At the end of ninety minutes neither side had found the net and extra time was called. It was then, somewhat unexpectedly, that Ian Winters, who had scored the winning goal for Gateshead against Liverpool in the 3rd round, put one past Bill Shortt and suddenly the dream was over. Gateshead marched on to draw Bolton Wanderers at Redheugh Park in the quarter-finals only to be sunk by a strike from the legendary Nat Lofthouse.

The following season it was a sadly familiar tale for Argyle: it wasn't until their eighth game that they recorded their first win, away at Swansea, and it wasn't until their seventh home match that they managed victory on their own turf. Ironically they scored the same number of goals as they had the previous season - 65 - but they conceded more, and rather than finish fourth from the top they finished fourth from the bottom, which was one place higher than they would finish in the following, 1954/55 season.

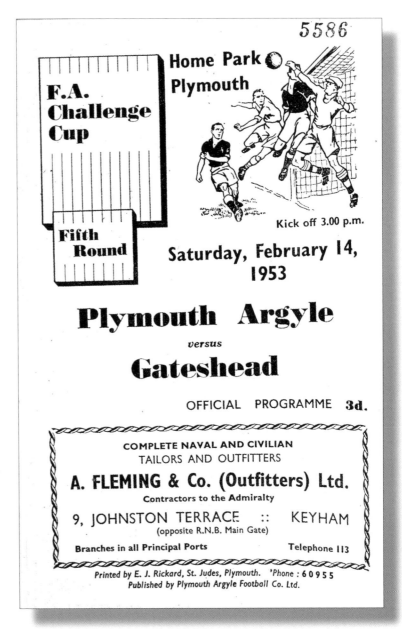

Valetine's day 1953 and Plymouth Argyle reach the dizzy heights of the fifth round of the FA Cup for the first time in their history. It was the first time too for Gateshead.

'The Minerva', George Phipps with his wife Bessie and various friends including Mr & Mrs Hooper and the landlady of the neighbouring 'Allenby Arms'.

SOCIAL LIFE

Throughout the season, and across the nation, football was, almost inevitably, one of the main talking points in everyday conversation, and footballers, although their pay perhaps wasn't commensurate with their status, where held in high regard, few higher than the legendary Stanley Matthews. When Argyle lost to Gateshead in 1953, and Gateshead lost to Bolton, it was Bolton who made it to the final where they met Matthews' team, Blackpool.

In one of the most talked about finals ever, Bolton, who were given an early lead by Nat Lofthouse, were 3-1 up with 25 minutes left to play. Then in one of the most remarkable Wembley fairy tale endings Matthews provided the crosses for two of the three goals that gave Blackpool victory and Stan Mortenson a hat trick with just seconds remaining on the clock. Despite Mortenson's unique achievement, it was the first and to date, last Wembley FA Cup Final hat trick, the encounter became known as the Matthews final and Stanley further enhanced his position as a national hero, a position that cigarette manufacturers Craven 'A' had been keen to exploit that season when, in December, they ran a massive newspaper campaign where 'football genius' Stanley Matthews said that Craven 'A' were 'the cigarette for me.'

There was, at the time, little thought that smoking was harmful and motor racing star Stirling Moss was another Craven 'A' fan – 'it gives me all I want from a smoke, and nothing I don't'. Most people, however, smoked Woodbines … and there was no getting away from it, as most people smoked: at work, at home, in the cinema, in the pub, on the buses and on the trains. One 1949 survey calculated that 79.1 per cent of the male population puffed, along with 37.7 per cent of the female population.

Top: *Servicemen had to wear uniforms on leave.*
Bottom: *Doreen and John Horne socialising inside the Pier Head Nissen hut at Coxside.*

Outside the 'Old Barley Sheaf' on the corner of Cambridge Street and King Street, note the Valente's ice cream hand cart.

There were no particular class boundaries, although the middle classes were more likely to smoke pipes and the working classes more likely to roll their own, but shops and newsagents routinely split packets and sold ciggies one or two at a time if asked and on average men smoked more than women (15 a day as opposed to a little under 7).

The percentages of people frequenting public houses was similar, a late-forties Mass Observation survey suggesting that 79 per cent of men and 49 per cent of women went to the pub. The figure for women was largely a product of the war: before 1939 very few women were seen in pubs, and it would appear that their presence had a significant effect on consumption. Prior to the First World War it was estimated that the annual per capita intake of beer was around 27.5 gallons, a figure that had virtually halved, to 14.2, by 1938 and which was down to 12.5 gallons by 1951-2. Of course that was still the best part of a pint a day for every beer-swilling adult.

Not that beer was all that people drank, but it was the most common drink, and many pubs were just beerhouses, where no spirits were sold. Bitter, mild, stout, mild and bitter, Guinness, brown ale and light ale were the most typical tipples, with women tending towards the stout until the arrival of the 'brilliantly marketed "champagne" perry, with the appealing Bambi deer symbol … which freed women from the dismal inexpensive alternatives of "*milk stout, sweet cider or the sickly VP wines*".' (David Kynaston *Family Britain 1951-57*)

Priced at 1/3d (6p), this was a welcome and affordable alternative, but heralded a general change in pub culture. For a start there were fewer and fewer pubs. There were dozens of closures across Plymouth, Stonehouse and Devonport in the first ten years after the war, mostly however, on account of redevelopment, nevertheless few of them were replaced.

Overall the typical regular was said to be male, married and over-25, working class, and earning somewhere between £4 and £6 per week. Darts, dominoes and shove ha'penny were among the most popular pub pastimes, along with bar billiards, crib and whist, but generally there seemed to be less singing and entertainment as punters could find that in their sports and social clubs or concert halls.

Setting out on a pub crawl/darts outing to Torbay from the Stoke Vaults c.1949.

The annual outing was another favoured focal point of the pub community and everything would be done to ensure the best use of time. Parties would assemble for an early morning departure with breakfast somewhere within in a twenty-mile range, before moving on to a lunchtime stop somewhere else, with maybe another stop before or after lunch. Tea would most likely be taken at yet another location, with a supper stop almost guaranteed before returning home a bit before midnight. With little or no opportunity for longer breaks away from home, these jollies were greatly appreciated. There would be much talk ahead of the event as the anticipation levels rose; great excitement and adventure on the day; and many hours of post-mortem, sharing stories of the day's events, long after it was over.

A large proportion of the population, particularly those without their own transport, were dependent on these outings for the opportunity to enjoy a short break from their everyday surroundings. Meanwhile, for those who could afford their own motorbike, or motor car, other possibilities opened up.

Although the motor car was still largely the preserve of the professional classes, there could be no denying that more and more families were availing themselves of four-wheeled freedom machines. In the first quarter of 1953 new car registrations were up to around 60,000, an increase of almost 50 per cent on the same period twelve months earlier. After some seven years of post-war austerity, where short-term solutions and day-to-day living had been the principal concern – epitomised by the amount of money the nation spent on drinking, smoking and entertainment – now it was possible to step back and take a look at the bigger picture.

Some things were still on ration, but food consumption, in the first seven months of 1953, was up 50 per cent on the same time two years previously and with more meat in the shops housewives were becoming increasingly fussy, and less inclined to hoover up anything that was on offer.

The times they were a-changing: television had yet to arrive this far west, but it was on its way; meanwhile, the voluptuous film star Gina Lollobrigida was photographed opening a coffee bar in Soho, heralding a new era for England's youth culture, and that same year, 1953, American entrepreneur, Eddie Gould, introduced his first Wimpy burger bar on these shores – in Wimbledon.

Locally meanwhile, Stafford Williams's popular Magnet Cafe in Whimple Street, and Stuart's Snack Bar on North Hill were at the forefront of the post-war generation of food and drink establishments that were slowly but surely transforming the face of the city.

Coach trips from the local: Top *outside the 'Ship Inn' on the Parade,* Middle: *outside the 'Dolphin', and* Bottom: *outside the 'Charlotte Street Ale Stores', Morice Town.* Right: *Stuart's Snack Bar, 1951.*

Picnic time: Albert Sandy – one of Plymouth's credit drapers – and his family tuck into an al fresco feast somewhere on the outskirts of town.

THE ARMED SERVICES

'Matelots used to get paid once a fortnight - cash. The first week all the pubs would be busy ... the second week it was the cider pubs that were busiest. At tuppence (1p) a pint, cider was the cheapest way to get drunk.' (Jim Luckie, a Union Street publican for almost fifty years)

Union Street had already achieved a degree of international notoriety long before the war, on a par with Bugis Street in Singapore and the Gut in Malta. Servicemen, particularly Bootnecks (Royal Marines) and Matelots, would attempt to drink their way from one end of the 'Strip' to the other and back. With a couple of dozen pubs along its length those achieving the feat were few and far between, even if they constrained themselves to a half in every hostelry.

Some were undoubtedly more popular than others: the Stonehouse Tavern - officially in Edgcumbe Street and the most westerly until the Earl Grey was rebuilt, was the generally the first port of call as the bus stop was right outside it. The tile-fronted Madeira Inn was another with a handily situated bus stop outside while across the road was the Jamaica House Inn and the West India House - the names themselves readily reflecting the jolly Jack Tar's Join-the-Navy-and-see-the-World experience. Indeed the latter was crammed full of souvenirs from all corners of the globe: there was a pickled Pygmy, thought to have been 'imported' by a merchant seaman, there was also a pickled elephant's 'wotsit', an ostrich egg, various swords, bayonets, helmets, assagai spears and busts of Wellington, Nelson and George V.

Opposite page: *Royal Parade in Coronation mode.*

Inside the 'West India House', Union Street with landlord Jim Luckie.

Tom Lingwood was the landlord here throughout the war years: a former wall-of-death rider in a circus show, he regularly entertained the circus folk when they were in town. The West India was one of the biggest pubs in the Street, indeed it was one of the biggest in the City and when Jim Luckie took over in 1953, he did so on condition that the brewery spent a small fortune refurbishing it first: *'It was a well-known rough cider pub. There was a big burner in the bar and the "scrumpy wallahs" would sit around, having eaten nothing, and from time to time the coke fumes would get to them and they'd just keel over flat out on the floor.'*

The brewery spent £25,000 on the face-lift, a massive amount for the time.

Another popular pub was the Sydenham Arms, just to the east of the Octagon (it has since been renamed the Clipper): here, in the late-forties, local artist and jazz musician Vincent Bennett painted a massive mural around the walls, its various vignettes providing an amusing insight into Union Street life at the time. A number of patrons were painted into the settings the overall effect affirming the Strip's prime attractions – the 'Three P's – Pubs, Prostitutes and the Paramount.

The Paramount was a small, first floor, dance-hall. It was a little on the rough side: *'It was always a laugh. I saw all the sights you are going to see, women fighting, prostitutes fighting. They used to throw you down the stairs. The MPs (Military Police) every night would park their truck at the bottom of the stairs - I once got involved in something and ended up going down the stairs as well. I found myself in one of the vans with a bruise on every one of the bones on my spine – I was in the right place at the wrong time.'* (Jimmy Farrell)

'The National Anthem was on the juke box and if fighting broke out in the club the barman would just stick it on and all the Servicemen would stop and stand to attention.' (Derek Tall)

The Paramount, with its trestle-table bar and limited range of spirits, was the only late-night (after 10pm) venue for some time and 'nice girls' didn't tend to go there. Much more dignified was the NAAFI (Navy, Army and Air Force Institute), this bar, dance hall and restaurant was housed for some years after the war in temporary accommodation alongside the ABC Royal.

Opposite page: *various views of the inside of the 'Sydenham Arms', Union Street, featuring Vincent Bennett's colourful and humorous mural.*

The NAAFI was temporarily housed in Nissen Huts alongside the ABC Royal Cinema.

The NAAFI in HMS Drake. *Inset: Summer of 1948, young apprentices at HMS Fisguard; Tom Mason, Brian Martin, and Des Robinson.*

This somewhat impromptu collection of Nissen Huts which had opened in 1945 was, in the summer of 1952, superseded by the opening of the new NAAFI in Notte Street, Princess Margaret arriving by aeroplane to open the building in her first official visit to the city.

The facilities offered by the new NAAFI were in a different league altogether to anything locally that had preceded it:

'The many amenities include a spacious ballroom with a modern cocktail bar in the gallery overlooking the dance floor – a large tavern – television lounge – comfortable lounge and writing room – games room (billiards, darts, table tennis and other games) – self service valet – barber's shop – WVS Information Bureau – sound-proof music and radio room – kiosk for sale of general goods and a supply of daily newspapers, magazines and periodicals.'

Plus 'a high-class cafeteria restaurant offering excellent meals at moderate prices' and, in Raleigh House, the residential wing, 'forty-two well-furnished double bedrooms each fitted with running hot and cold water, offering the Servicemen and his wife first-class accommodation at very reasonable rates'. There were also, incidentally, seven bedrooms reserved for members of the Women's Services.

And jolly reasonable the charges were too: 12/6d (62p) per day for a double room for the first six days and 10 shillings a day (50p) thereafter.

Top left: *Princess Margaret opens the new NAAFI facility in Notte Street.*
Top right: *Inside the new venue.*
Above, left and right: *Illustrations of the ballroom and a typical bedroom.*
Right: *The exterior decorated for the Coronation.*

Princess Margaret's visit in 1952 may have been her first official solo appearance in the city, but it certainly wasn't the first time she had been here, having toured HMS *Duke of York* at Devonport Dockyard shortly after the war, with her elder sister, Princess Elizabeth.

There were, as it transpired, plenty of visitors to the Dockyard in the late forties, thanks to the revival, in 1948, of Naval Week, rebranded and slightly shortened as Navy Days.

With the war still fresh in many minds, there was a great appetite for people wanting to step on board a warship and with little going on in the way of post-war ship-building most exhibits were war veterans of one kind or another.

There had been a particularly busy and intense period of ship-building before the war – some two dozen ships in ten years – and while work continued through the war, as the end of the conflict came into sight so, various projects were either put on the back burner or cancelled:

HMS *Ace* was one such casualty. An Amphion class submarine, she was actually laid down on 3 December 1943 and launched on 14 March 1945, however the vessel was never completed. Instead her hull was used for crush depth-testing before she was taken from Devonport to Glasgow for breaking up in the summer of 1950.

As it transpired, it wasn't until a few weeks after the Coronation of the former Princess Elizabeth that Devonport saw another home-grown ship launched.

Laid down on the first day of the previous year, 1 January 1952, HMS *Salisbury* (F32) was the first all-welded ship to have been built at Devonport. Constructed on a pre-fabricated principle, *Salisbury* was also the Royal Navy's first new Type 61 aircraft-direction frigate.

Launched by the wife of the then Commander in Chief, Admiral Sir Maurice Mansergh, *Salisbury* had a displacement of over 2,000 tons, was 100 metres long and was eventually signed off as completed early in 1959.

The immediate post-war period was a comparatively quiet time for the Dockyard: two of the biggest jobs being the repairs to 8,258 ton US Lines craft *American Farmer* and the Norwegian-owned *Athel Duchess*.

The former was brought here in July 1946 having collided with her sister ship *William J Riddle* and was repaired in just under 50 days. Meanwhile the 13,000-ton tanker, *Athel Duchess*, came here after being holed by a mine off the Bay of Biscay at the end of 1946. A price for her repair was proffered, but the work took much longer and costs spiralled to almost double the original quote of £250,000 by the time work had been completed in June 1948.

The Admiralty tried for almost a year to extract a contribution from the vessel's owners to offset the loss, but to no avail. In the end the authorities were philosophical about the fact that at least there had been work to do and by the time the fixed overheads had been taken account of the overall loss was probably only about £40,000.

Top left: Princesses Elizabeth and Margaret Rose on board HMS Duke of York.
Right: Launch of HMS Salisbury, 1953. Opposite page, top: Dockyard and Warships.

November 1949 HMS Amethyst receives a hero's welcome at Devonport - inset one of the many printed picture souvenir accounts of the Amethyst's escapade.

Not surprisingly, under the circumstances, there were frequent 'slack' periods in the yard and, after six years or war and ten years of build up prior to that, few moments of great excitement, hence the fanfares that greeted the return of HMS *Amethyst* in November 1949.

With a Civil War raging in China, where the Nationalists were fighting the Communists, both Britain and America, although not directly involved, had supplied hardware, including ships, to the Chinese Government - who were the Nationalists.

On 20 April 1949 HMS *Amethyst* was charged with the task of sailing up the Yangtze River to the British Embassy at Nanking to relieve the guard ship there, HMS *Consort*. Her role partly to be on standby in case there was a sudden need to evacuate British and Commonwealth nationals from the area. It did not look like being an especially easy passage as recently there had been bitter fighting between the Nationalists on the south side of the river and the Communists to the north. However, with the blessing of the Chinese Government, and with a large Union Jack hung on either side of the ship, *Amethyst* made her way slowly up river.

On the night of 19 April, she anchored at Kiang Yin for the night. Also in port at that time were five Nationalist warships, under threat of fire from the Communists on the north bank. It would appear, however, that as long as they remained at anchor, the Communists had agreed not to attack them.

It has since been suggested, therefore, that when the *Amethyst* continued up river the next morning, the Communists took her to be one of the Nationalist ships breaking out of port and opened fire on her, notwithstanding the presence of those Union Jacks.

Seventeen crewmen were killed and two more died subsequently of their injuries. Doubtless in the interests of not being provocative *Amethyst* was only armed with practice shells and it was some time before high explosives could be brought up from below, by which time two gun turrets were out of action and the ship had gone aground on a sandbank.

Consort came straight down from Nanking to help, but was herself fired on and lost ten of her crew. Not in a position to stop, *Consort* carried on down the river, all guns blazing.

HMS **Black Swan** and HMS *London* were then detailed to provide assistance, but they too came under attack, suffered casualties, and were compelled to abandon the attempt.

The British Press were outraged and while the debate on who exactly had started what went on, the British Government refused to sign up to any conciliatory agreement that involved them admitting to something they deemed to be untrue.

And so *Amethyst* was stranded. Weeks went by. Conditions deteriorated. Food and fuel stocks got low. The heat became unbearable for the skeleton crew on board, but the rats and cockroaches had a field day. The weeks became months and with diplomacy getting nowhere, the man put in to command the *Amethyst*, Commander Kerans, with the covert blessing of Admiral Brind of the Far East Station, decided to make a bid for escape.

On 30 July 1949 in the knowledge it would be a largely moon-less night, they slipped anchor – having packed the anchor chain with greased wadding to deaden the sound and made, with a scare or two along the way, a daring escape – one which captured the imagination of the world and which, eight years later, was the subject of a film starring Richard Todd as Kerans and featuring *Amethyst* as herself.

Dockside reception, 1949 - eight years later Amethyst would be broken up in Sutton Harbour.

Royal Army Service Corps – Chief Engineers and Skippers: Among them Captain Ferris (4th from left front row), Vittle and Wilkinson (front row), Houghton and Aldridge (second row) and Turner (back row). Far right top: Amiens *towing a target in the Sound. Bottom left: The* Blue Peter *alongside* Cronach, *and right: The* Blue Peter *with Tom McKnight, Skipper..*

Locally it wasn't just the Navy who were taking to the water; there was also the Royal Army Service Corps, a unit that operated out of a Nissen hut at Coxside. Operating a fleet of five MTBs (Motor Torpedo Boats) around the port, all commanded by retired naval officers, the RASC ferried fuel, supplies and personnel hither and thither – to Mount Batten. Drake's Island, Turnchapel, Fort Picklecombe and Cawsand.

These harbour launches were a familiar sight around the waterfront and were regularly deployed in the dicey business of towing targets around the Sound as target practice for the big guns at Lentney (one of the batteries of HMS *Cambridge* at Wembury).

'One launch would clear the area and another launch would have a target behind it at the end of a 1,000-yard cable – sometimes they had night shoots. And sometimes they came a bit close!

'The launches could move at quite a speed, over 30 knots, although at that speed we'd be burning about two gallons of petrol a minute.'
(Len McVicar - a former MTB skipper who started as a boy seaman at the age of fourteen and a half)

Cumberland Battery c.1950, inside the Citadel.

As well as the RASC on the eastern side of Sutton Harbour there was also the CAS – Coastal Artillery School, later the 47th Coast Regiment – who were stationed, just after the war, firstly at Turnchapel (Mount Stamford Barracks) and then at the Royal Citadel.

As well as the living accommodation provided inside the Citadel there was an imposing terrace of married quarters on the southern side of Lambhay Hill.

Post-war the Citadel remained an important base, while Stamford and neighbouring Mount Batten, were of declining significance, the later making the longest exit.

The long-serving Australian No.10 Squadron left for their home on the other side of the world on 31 October 1945 – they had completed over 3,000 operations from Mount Batten, during the course of which they had sunk a number of German U-Boats. Their departure was lamented by the many friends they had made here, as well as a generation of schoolboys who had delighted in watching the Sunderland flying-boats taking off and landing on the waters around the Sound.

Top: *Sergeants Warefield and Tom Daley in a staff car, 1947* Above: *MT (Motor Transport) section 1947: Fosbrook, Charlton, Bennett, Knowles, Banbury and Ashton.* Right: *Outside married quarters on Lambhay Hill c.1950*

Other uniformed units around the town included a still-significant Army presence – at Seaton Barracks and Plumer Barracks - both at Crownhill. The former being named after one of the heroes of the Battle of Waterloo, John Colborne, later Lord Seaton, who was well known in the area and who retired near Plympton, the latter named after Torquay-born Field Marshall, Lord Plumer.

Crownhill Fort, the principal structure of the ring of 22 Palmerston forts surrounding the Three Towns, was incidentally still in military occupation throughout the forties and fifties, while Raglan Barracks, at Devonport, which had been reprieved on the outbreak of war, served as headquarters for some of Plymouth's Territorial and Auxiliary Force Unit.

Plans to demolish Raglan had already been set in motion and work on razing South Raglan had just begun when war broke out and put an end to the proceedings. The barracks were also used to house a Civil Service department.

At Stonehouse, the Royal Marines were as strong as ever and in 1951 the thirty-year-old Duke of Edinburgh, a graduate of the Royal Naval College at Dartmouth, came to Stonehouse to present new colours to the Plymouth Division and four years later, on the occasion of their 200th Anniversary, the City granted the Royal Marine Corps the Freedom of the City.

As ever, such events were marked by marching parades, through the city and most notably on the Hoe, where great numbers turned out to see the ever-popular Royal Marine Band and witness the celebrations surrounding the monarch's birthday and other official occasions.

ROYAL TOURNAMENT 1954

The return of a successful Field Gun Crew from the Royal Tournament was always a good pretext for such an event and in the early fifties Devonport dominated the competition.

For five consecutive years they brought the Interport Challenge trophy back to Plymouth (although they actually shared the title with Portsmouth in 1955) at the same time they also won the Aggregate Time Challenge and, with one exception (in 1951 when Chatham won it), the Fastest Time cup.

Top: *426 Squadron of the ATC at Raglan Barracks with Roy Todd and Richard Hill.*
Above: *Devonport Field Gun Team 1952 Triple trophy winners.*

Left: *March past of nearly 2,000 officers and men of the Royal Navy, Army and RAF on Queen Elizabeth's first birthday parade.* Top right: *Major-General JE Leech-Porter, Commandant Royal Marines, Plymouth, making his first inspection.* Bottom right: *Boer War veterans parading on the Hoe, 1949.*

Plymouth Police force c.1950 (both motorbikes were registered 1947/8)

There was a degree of antipathy between two of the uniformed services on 29 July 1945 when the City Police were asked to escort the President of the United States through the city to Millbay to be taken out to meet King George VI on HMS *Renown*, in Plymouth Sound.

Fog prevented the President's plane from being able to put down as planned at RAF St Mawgan and instead, amid fears that the Skymaster plane transporting him was too big to land at Harrowbeer, the aircraft successfully touched down. President Truman was by this stage over an hour ahead of schedule and Chief Constable John Skittery, who was responsible for the security arrangements advised that the President remain on his plane until they could re-establish the original timetable.

'For reasons I never fathomed, this waiting period proved too much for the FBI bodyguard. Less than half an hour had passed when the senior member of the FBI team informed me that we must start for Plymouth. He contended that the waiting period entailed too great a security risk for the president.

'The head of the FBI party had been in touch with an American landing-craft base at Victoria Wharf and for some obscure reason it was felt that the President's safety would be better taken care of if he embarked from there instead of from Millbay.

'Police wireless facilities then were not as they exist today and there was no way of warning the Lord Mayor or the public of the alterations to the original plan.

'When we arrived at Victoria Wharf a very irate Commander-in-Chief (Sir Ralph Leatham), who had just been able to get there a moment or two after the President's arrival seemed to think that the change of plan was my fault, but there was no time to explain as he forced his way through a mass of American sailors to meet Mr Truman.

'There were no open tourers (so our men can have a clear view of all windows above street level) in the car procession into the city, but in front and behind Mr Truman's car were two United States Army jeeps, in which an over-large number of gentlemen in very large hats, who were no doubt very adequately armed, maintained a precarious foothold.' (John Skittery, Chief Constable, quoted in *Rattles to Radio*) The security arrangements for the King were much more low key.

Top: *Sir Ralph Leatham, His Majesty King George VI, President Truman and James F Byrnes, US Secretary of State on board* Renown. Above: *Police highway code demostration c.1950.*

Eileen Normington, the first regular policewoman attached to Plymouth City Police Force.

John Skittery had been appointed Chief Constable here in 1943 and he remained in post throughout the forties and fifties, during which time he was responsible for a number of measures that put the Plymouth force at the forefront of British policing.

'Regular wireless patrols started on January 1 1946 on a sixteen hours a day basis and as the cars were crewed by advanced drivers, four minutes was quickly established as the maximum time for a car and observer to reach any part of the city. And how effective it all was. In the fullness of time all vehicles were equipped with wireless and cover was complete throughout the twenty four hours. Lightweight motorcycles were used for the larger beats in the northern part of the city, the riders being affectionately known as "Skittery's Light Horse".' (Ernest Dickaty, *From Rattles To Radio*)

The number of women within the force was increasing during this time too. During the war there were six attested members of the Women's Auxiliary Police Corps, but only one served in that capacity. At the dawn of 1946 out of a constabulary of 314 there were but three women, each of whom wore *'uniform of a more or less standard police design. 'They were now obviously a part of the force and in 1953 there was a further increase, this time of a sergeant and three constables.'* (ibid)

Plymouth's first woman sergeant, incidentally, was Mildred Cooper, from Walsall (she would later become the first woman inspector).

The matter of uniform was another area in which Skittery made some pioneering moves, viz Memo dated 17 July 1951:

'At the discretion of superintendents, which discretion may be delegated to any of your inspectors, constables and sergeants, can be permitted, if they so desire, to do duty on the streets in shirt-sleeve order – with the following provisos.

1 Sleeves are to be carefully rolled up to just above the elbow.

2 Belted-type trousers only can be worn without tunics.

3 Careful attention is paid to collars and ties in order to see that they are smart and clean.

4 The pocket book and pencil can be carried in a hip pocket.

5 Whistles are to be carried in the trouser pocket.

6 Truncheons will be carried normally.

7 Shirt-sleeve order can only be worn between 8am and 8pm

8 It is understood that all men parading for duty will bring their tunics with them. Under no circumstances are tunics to be left in police boxes.'

Another area where the Chief Constable was relatively relaxed was with regard to motoring infringements with '*motorists invariably getting a warning for first offences where minor traffic laws had been breached.*'
Skittery also allowed people to park their cars at night without lights, in places where the street lighting was deemed to be adequate.

Of the other emergency services the immediate post-war period was notable for the number of different craft that served as the City's Lifeboat:
The *Minstre Anseele* a German-built, Belgian lifeboat had been found drifting and crewless off Weymouth in September 1940 and was brought around to Plymouth in February 1943. In 1946 she was returned to the Belgian Government and the 22-year-old vessel *The Brothers*, served for little under a year before being replaced by the *Robert and Marcella Beck*. That in turn was sold off in 1952 and superseded by the brand new *Thomas Forehead and Mary Rowse*, which was donated by Miss Mary Rowse of Birmingham. Her donation of £40,000 was one of the largest that the RNLI had ever received, and the splendid vessel was officially named by the Duchess of Kent on Friday 16 May 1952.
The boat was to become a familiar sight over the next 22 years, during which time its crew would save over 60 lives.

As for the Fire Service, there were, in the post-war period, three fire stations within the then Plymouth boundary:
At the Headquarters at Greenbank: with another at Molesworth Road, Stoke and a third at The Drive, at the top of Hartley.
Curiously enough, anyone calling in the event of an emergency had to dial 999 from a public phone box, but 2222 from a private house or business number.

Left: A memorial plaque to Plymouth's Firemen is unveiled.
Above: Champagne christening for Plymouth's new lifeboat "Thomas Forehead and Mary Rowse." The lifeboat, given by Miss A Charlton Rowse of Birmingham, was named by the Duchess of Kent.

Devasted Devonport, looking east towards the Market, St John the Baptist and Devonport Column.

DEVONPORT AND DEVELOPMENT

Devonport's Blitz had come a month after the Luftwaffe had laid waste to Plymouth City Centre: here the devastation had been equally intense and once the dust had settled it was clear that there were few areas that had been left untouched. Once all the burnt-out shells had been demolished it was equally clear that there would need to be a major rethink.

Initially, after all the rubble was cleared, the big open spaces that were left readily lent themselves to short-term occupation by some of the American units that came across the Atlantic to join in the war effort. Row upon row of Nissen huts were erected either side of Fore Street, but these were not for shops, as they were in Plymouth, but rather, for the most part anyway, for the accommodation of supplies and servicemen. It was a different situation to that prevailing in Plymouth, but then Devonport had always been based around the Armed Services and this was important not just to the immediate neighbourhood, but to the City as a whole:

'The Future of this city, and particularly the Devonport area, is dependent upon the maintenance of a Grand Fleet, the necessity for which is bound up with the political and international picture structure of the Allied Nations in the years after the war. He would be a bold person who would be dogmatic on such a subject with world events and conditions changing as they have done during the past few years.' (Plan for Plymouth, 1943)

Looking north from the Column towards Fore Street, with three survivors among the Nissen Huts - Burtons, the Midland Bank and Marks and Spencer.

185

Devonport from the air in 1949 with Marlborough Street running left to right in the middle distance, towards St Paul's Church, its tower still standing on St Morice Square.

Of course the authors of the Plan, which was written fully two years before the end of the war, were quite right, nobody could quite predict how the global picture would shape up once the war had ended. And therein lay a massive problem for Devonport and the Admiralty. How big a Dockyard were they going to need after the war? The big decision-makers were all of an age where they could remember what happened after the last Great War, how work in the yard had gradually been scaled down after ten years had passed, and then, as Germany started to re-arm, so the programme of works in the Dockyard was cranked up again and in little more than 20 years after armistice we were at war again.

And so it was that the decision-makers dithered.

After early indications that they would want to acquire some 240 acres of dockside land after the war, the Admiralty eventually asked Plymouth City Council if they would acquire 182 acres. However, three years later and with little activity in the meantime, they announced that over the next twelve years they would require just 154 acres. The following year they cut that almost in two and said that 78.5 acres would suffice: then, in March 1955, the Admiralty released 17 acres of that allocation: *'the reduction being thought due to modern warfare's need to avoid excessive industrial concentration.'* (Lt-Cdr Ken Burns, *The Devonport Dockyard Story*)

In the meantime, the economy of Devonport and the community within Devonport struggled. Blitzed shops and entertainment centres were not replaced, everyone was expected to make do with those places that survived, or go into Plymouth itself. As the Admiralty started firming up its plans the situation became even more difficult.

The two florists – Hearl's and Crosley's – who had been occupying the old Devonport Market building, moved out in May 1954 – the former going to Cumberland Street, the latter to Ordnance Street. That same month Marks & Spencers closed their Fore Street premises and transferred their staff and stock to their new Plymouth branch. Earlier that year the Plymouth Co-operative Society had cleared its tailoring shop out of Marlborough Street, and its confectionary outlet in Morice Street. Sometime later Perkin Brothers, the long-established outfitters, and specialists in school blazers, caps and badges, closed down and when that once-great champion of Devonport, Sir Clifford Tozer, moved his stores out of Devonport and into the new Plymouth City Centre, the chances of the old town maintaining any credible commercial heart were slim indeed.

27 July 1951 aerial view of South Western Gas Board's Devonport Unit - the coke works obliquely opposite the Royal Naval Engineering College. In the river we see the cruiser Nigeria *and, midstream, the destroyer D204, PNS Tughril (formerly HMS* Onslaught) *and in the No.3 basin, L14 - HMS* Beaufort.

The familiar landmarks of St Aubyn Church and Raglan gatehouse point up to and through the skyline, with Market Street running down towards the former, Barrack Street in the direction of the latter and Edinburgh Road, Catherine Street, Tavistock Street and St Aubyn Street all criss-crossing them.

Gradually Fore Street was cleared and earmarked for different Dock-yard uses. In 1954 signs started appearing here and there: between Fore Street, Chapel Street, Cumberland Street and Catherine Street, their stark message: 'Keep Out – Admiralty Property'.

Chaplin's Pickle Factory, and the Union Savings Bank both disappeared – although the latter was to be rebuilt in the New Welcome Building in the surviving section of Fore Street.

St Paul's Church, Morice Square was demolished, while St Stephen's, which, like St John the Baptist had partially survived, and St Mary the Virgin, which had survived unscathed, were all doomed.

The rationale was that the ecclesiastical needs of the area could now be served by St Aubyn Church in Chapel Street and so the parishes of St Stephen's, St Mary's, St Paul's, and St John the Baptist, were merged into one, and the Reverend JH Jones, was appointed to over-see the newly merged congregations.

Meanwhile, a former aircraft hangar from the RAF station at Harrow-beer was pressed into divine service in Fore Street as a new Central Hall for the local Methodists.

And at the same time as that oppressive great wall started to go up around, what would become known as the Dockyard's 'Storage Enclave' a number of other once-prominent landmarks were removed, along with a large number of pubs, among them the Elephant and Castle, Post Office Inn, Volunteer Inn and Butcher's Arms.

Ever a vital community asset of sorts, there had been 100 pubs within the confines of old Devonport at the end of the First World War. Within 20 years of the end of the Second World War, however, that number was to drop to just 21 – 'two of which' it was noted, 'possess eating facilities.'.

A new road linking old Devonport to the massive pre-war developments to the North of the town was proposed, cutting through Devonport Park from the top of Chapel Street, through Granby Barracks, and along Garden Street into Albert Road and impressive plans were drawn up for big new blocks of flats to the north and south of the area being walled off.

Housing was a really pressing priority right across the city after the war and before more permanent solutions could be constructed in Devonport, a line of American-type pre-fabs was erected along the western side of King's Road. Overall, though, ten years after the war had ended, Devonport was still in a very sorry state.

Top: *Two of the many pubs that disappeared - Rose and Crown and the Butchers.* Middle: *A former RAF Harrowbeer hangar is pressed into service as a temporary home for Central Hall, Fore Street (it opened in May 1950).* Bottom: *American-style pre-fabs in King's Road.*

The ancient 'Spread Eagle' tavern in Treville Street, a wartime survivor but destined to be a casualty of the redevelopment.

However, while Devonport's post-war story was undoubtedly a sad one and one that saw the new City Centre grow at Devonport's expense, there was still plenty to grieve about in old Plymouth itself.

Before the war the local authority had embarked on a mission to rid the most ancient parts of town of its slums. That work had been interrupted by the war and it is remarkable to note that in the ten years before the war and in the ten years after the war, the City Council pulled down more Tudor and Jacobean buildings in Plymouth than the Luftwaffe managed to destroy during the Blitz.

Part of the driving force for this activity after the war was the fact that a Government licence was granted to local authorities to build a new house every time an old house was pulled down. This policy led to the almost wanton destruction of many delightful old buildings around Sutton Harbour - in Notte Street, High Street, Vauxhall Street, Exeter Street, off Lambhay Hill, and Castle Street - all well outside the perimeter of the bold new City Centre.

People were starting to get more vocal in expressing their concerns. An architect, Mr Z Bienawski, working in the City Architect's department, dismayed by those seeking *'to throw overboard all sentiments for history and tradition, and to modernise the area to meet purely economical and housing needs of New Plymouth'* put forward another option altogether: *'to rehabilitate the old City with enlightened respect to her history and her characteristic Town Scape, yet in conformity with contemporary standards of living so that she may pursue her sound traditional life AND attract visitors and win their affection.'*

Sadly his very detailed report, submitted in 1954 and examining the worth of every Barbican building still standing, was overlooked, as was the 1951 Schedule of Listed Buildings, the 1948 report from the Society for the Protection of Ancient Buildings, and a more recent report from the Fine Art Commission, not to mention the informed and by no means fanciful suggestions from the Old Plymouth Society, the Plymouth Institution, and the Port of Plymouth Chamber of Commerce. There was no doubt that certain members of the Council were being incredibly cavalier in their attitude towards the heritage of the City and to the opinions of those whose views were normally valued.

The bottom line, inevitably, was a financial one: *'Preservation costs money and would mean the loss of a subsidy,'* warned Miller, while Bert Medland added, *'it all boils down to how much money you are prepared to pay for the preservation of a lot of rubbish down on the Barbican.'*

Small wonder that one councillor proposed that the City's coat of arms be amended to *'two bulldozers rampant on a sea of rubble'.*

Top: *The late-Victorian artisans' buildings in Notte Street.* Bottom left: *No.s 1-3 Vauxhall Street.* Bottom right: *The junction of High Street and the Parade - all wartime survivors, all, unfortunately, casualties of the redevelopment.*

In the event a compromise was reached and the legislation amended to allow certain old buildings to be kept and licences issued for new buildings, as long as the old buildings in question were not used for domestic purposes, that is as long as no one was living in them.

The Plymouth Barbican Association, initially an offshoot of the Old Plymouth Society spearheaded a high-profile campaign which was supported by Nancy Astor and the poet laureate, John Betjamin.

In time it would transform the Barbican into a bustling community of artists, craftsmen and an interesting range of small businesses.

Meanwhile, the pressing problem of rehousing thousands of Plymothians continued to tax the local authorities. This was where the newly elected Labour Council threw the bulk of their resources at the situation. It was the first time that they had been in control of the Council and by 1949 they were able to proudly announce that '18,900 persons, representing 5,730 families have been housed in new properties'.

Of these 878 completed houses and flats were on the Efford Estate (which had been laid out for 924 properties):

'This is the third largest estate developed by the Housing Committee, providing homes for approximately 3,000 people. It commands unrivalled views of the Plym estuary.'

At Ham 462 out of an aspirational 530 houses had already been completed and occupied. The second largest estate, situated to the north and south of the St Budeaux to Crownhill Road, Honicknowle and Woodland was over 80 per cent completed (760 out of 904 houses), while the largest of the immediate post-war estates – Ernesettle – was well on the way:

'The building of houses is in full swing: and the occupation of the first houses completed. The Bush Radio factory has been erected and is in production, already employing approximately 300 persons. This estate will proved for 1,204 houses and flats, and will accommodate approximately 4,000 people.'

If these statistics sound improbable at first glance it is worth remembering that up until 1949 there had been no real major construction work in the Blitzed City Centre and also a lot (some 2,250) of the new flats and houses were prefabricated properties.

Many of the prefabs had come from the United States, indeed more over half a million, most of them made by the American motor industry, were sent across to war-torn Europe in the forties.

Opposite page: Pramwheeis and planks create a makeshift cart on this typical post-war prefab estate.

Above: *Two views of Tamar Way (along the line of the planned Parkway). Bottom: showing junction with Little Dock Lane.*

Work on the 150-acre split site (the green space was reserved as an amenity) began in December 1945, just a few months after the end of the war and a few weeks after the Labour Party had taken over control of Plymouth City Council. Note the Carmelite Convent at the back of Thames Gardens. Inset: The view from the garden of Gainsborough Place, looking out over the bungalows of Romney Walk, with the Honicknowle brickworks chimeny in the distance.

The first British consignment had arrived in 1944. Locally many of these easy-to-erect structures occupied sites that had been cleared by German or Italian prisoners of war, *'who also constructed the roads, steps, paths and concrete foundations.'* (Barry Henderson)

Offering some 616 square-feet they measured roughly 19 feet by 21 feet, plus a rear and side entrance lobby.

Ergonomically designed, they had two bedrooms (10ft by 9ft and 9ft square) a lounge (10 by 12) and kitchen and bathroom and at the time, *'they proved to be very substantial and desirable dwellings'*.

For many of the families moving into these magnolia and green decorated bungalows it was the first time they had had a proper bathroom, indoor facilities – a fridge – and proper heating.

'You lit the coal fire in the sitting room and the heat filled the house … and fuelled the hot water system for the house. We'd never had a bathroom before … or a garden.

'To encourage people to look after their gardens there was an annual gardening competition. My dad grew all sorts of vegetables.

'The corrugated contraption at the top of the garden - we all had one: they were unused Anderson shelters - was used to store coal and gardening tools.' (Jean Perkins née Gray)

Jean and Mavis Gray outside their prefab in Shenstone Gardens

Above: *Two views of post-war Ernesettle, the second (bottom) from 1954 showing the estate almost fully formed with the school at the hub of the new community.*

Clockwise from top left: *Louis De Soissons designed houses; four old people's flats; Easi-Form - three-bedroom houses; Cornish Unit semi-detached.*

Of course not all of the new housing was of a prefabricated nature, and it was recognised that the prefab was only a temporary solution - typically they were reckoned to have a ten to fifteen year lifespan (most were to go on well beyond that!). Plymouth's 2,250 prefabs represented a small percentage of the national total (which was over 156,000), but accounted for almost half the Council-built programme up to 1949.

Post 1949 the plan was to put up another 4,729 houses, many of them scheduled to go on the newest and largest of the post-war estates - Whitleigh.

Overall, across the country there were some 1,200,000 new homes built in the first six years after the war and the vast majority were designed to last a lot longer than the prefab. However, even these tended to be stock designs that could be erected with comparative speed and ease.

Indeed one such off-the-shelf model, that became a common sight locally, was the Laing Easi-Form house: these two storey properties had cavity walls formed of two 3-inch layers of concrete (cast on site) separated by a 2-inch gap, with four horizontal reinforcing bands running around the house above and below the windows on each floor.

Another of the quick build units was the BISF house. Formed in 1934, the British Iron and Steel Federation – an association of steel producers – was constituted to co-ordinate production across the country and with the advent of war became a key player in addressing the post-blitz housing situation across the country.

Architect Sir Frederick Gibberd designed the classic BISF house, with two different cladding finishes to the upper and lower storeys (typically brick or steel to the lower section, timber weatherboard to the upper) and projecting window surrounds housing steel-framed Crittall Hope windows. Around 1,000 of these had been built on Plymouth's new estates by 1949, while during the same time-period some 1,500 brick-built homes were erected, most following the blueprints of architect Louis De Soissons.

There were also a significant number of Cornish Unit houses, designed by architects Beresford and Tonkin for the Central Cornwall Concrete and Artificial Stone Co. These too had a distinctive difference between the upper and lower part of the building, the upper part invariably being contained within a medium-pitched Mansard roof.

Over 30,000 of these houses were eventually produced and many of them found their way into Plymouth. However, timber construction of the upper part over the concrete frame created the potential for long term problems, as the two materials had a tendency to part company and cause cracking. The incorporation of asbestos in the wall and roof insulation was also to lead to long-term difficulties. But that was all in the future, for the time being Plymouth could be proud of its achievements, much of it down to the hard work and determination of Councillor Bill Miller.

The 55-year-old had become Chairman of the City Council's Housing Committee in November 1945 and his tireless efforts to rehouse the blitzed and bombed-out people of Plymouth saw him honoured with the BEM (British Empire Medal) in 1946, the OBE in 1947 and the CBE in 1948. During that time Bill, popularly known as 'Darkie', Miller turned down the chance to be Lord Mayor of the City on the grounds that he would have had to have surrendered his position on the Housing Committee. Miller made friends everywhere and pulled as many strings as he could: at one point he even had Dockyard workers making drainpipes, stoves and other items that were in short supply.

Remarkably, in relation to its overall population, Plymouth's record was only bettered by two other authorities.

Minister of Health, Aneurin Bevan, visits the City to open the first of the new Cornish Unit houses at Honicknowle, 17 June 1947, with the Chairman of Plymouth Housing Committee, Ald Bill Miller.

The new estates were not, of course, the only area in which homes were being created, there were also blocks of flats going up here and there – star-shaped developments on the Barbican, West Hoe, and Pennycomequick, and other developments like Athlone House, off Union Place which was opened on 27 November 1950.

It was good news for many who in some cases had been waiting almost ten years to once again have a home of their own. Mr and Mrs George Reed with their two children were the first to move in to the flats, their three-bedroomed Corporation accommodation costing them 30s 4d (152p) per week. Princess Alice, Countess of Athlone, was welcomed by Mrs Reed as the Princess and her husband presided over the opening ceremony. Lady Astor was there too as was the Lord Mayor, Mrs Jacquetta Marshall, Plymouth's first female Lord Mayor.

It was an impressive occasion and other dignitaries included Miller's successor on the Housing Committee, Harold Pattinson and representatives of the contractors, AN Coles and the architects, Louis de Soissons. Said Mr Pattinson, somewhat enigmatically: *'It is well known locally that this has been a very costly venture, but we have learned much from it and we must remember that everything must not be counted in terms of money, but in health and happiness as well.'*

Two of the news streets on the Ham Estate, both named after towns with Abbeys: Dryburgh Crescent and (bottom) Malmesbury Close - note the complete absence of motorcars.

Princess Alice, Countess of Athlone, at the opening of Athlone House (Union Street), 27 November 1950.

Ham Drive, a quiet new road cuts through the developing Ham Estate.

Top: *The newly laid out Crownhill Road running east-west across the top of the City.*
Bottom: *Lamplighters Henry Dann leads a group that includes his brother, Frederick.*

With so much of the immediate post-war building work being executed by Local Authorities up and down the country, it is interesting to note that by 1951 some 15 per cent of the residences in the country were now publicly owned, a higher percentage than existed in the Soviet Union at that time.

Not all of the post-war house-building was conducted by local authorities, however, but it did account for most if it: in that same post-war period, 1945-49, only 16 new houses were built locally through private enterprise, although some 610 private house-owners had their war-damaged properties rebuilt.

Unsurprisingly, a natural consequence of creating all these new housing estates was the call for more schools, community centres, health centres, shops and services.

Already, by 1949 some 28 miles of new roads had been laid around the city, along with 55.5 miles of sewers and countless miles of gas piping and electric cabling to provide power for heating, lighting and an ever-increasing range of domestic appliances: vacuum cleaners, spin-dryers, toasters – most of them requiring a source of electricity.

Remarkably enough, however, not all post-war properties had power points in every room and many were they who, generally oblivious to the dangers, plugged their early electric irons, radios and even television sets into the (unearthed) electric light pendant in the middle of the room.

However, although the electric lightbulb was rapidly taking over from the fragile gas mantle as the main form of in-house illumination, there was still a major battle between gas and electricity providers for lighting the streets.

Clearly, any form of street lighting was to be welcomed after the dark days and nights of the war and the years of blacked out windows and white-striped lampposts and kerbstones.

Historically the streets of England had been lit by candles, or oil lamps, or some other solid lighting source with a wick. Gradually, however, gas became the preferred form of street lighting, and across the towns and villages of England a small army of lamplighters would take to the streets at dusk to light the lamps, returning with their long poles at dawn, to turn the same lamps out. Locally at least the lamplighters had to provide their own wicks and matches and on wet and windy nights it wasn't unknown for a lamplighter to get through several boxes of matches.

Above left: Corner of Edgar Terrace, a new electric light towers above an old gas light, Mr J Agg and Mr C Thomas both of SWEB, look on. Right: An Electricity Board, Bedford Hawson lorry in Emma Place, Stonehouse and (bottom) a forties' South Western Gas Board (Plymouth and North Cornwall) van.

Gasmen at work c.1950.

By the dawn of the 1950s, though, Plymouth's last 1,100 gas lamps had been refashioned to work with time clocks, prompting the end of an era for the old lamplighter and promoting the viability of gas in the face of increasing competition from the clean simplicity of electricity.

Low pressure sodium and high-pressure mercury lighting had started finding favour over gas lighting before the war and, interestingly enough, Plymouth Pier had been one of the first major places in Plymouth to be 'lighted by electricity' as far back as 1884, but the switch to electricity generally took place over several decades (for example electric street lighting first reached Radford and Hooe in the early 1930s).

In the immediate post-war period the Plymouth Division of the then newly formed South Western Gas Board (which took over the Plymouth and Stonehouse Gas Light & Coke Company and its Devonport neighbour on 1 May 1949) and the South Western Electricity Board each went to great lengths to demonstrate the efficacy of their particular power supply, taking photographs of their installations by night and day.

The nationalisation of the Gas Board incidentally, mirrored the nationalisation of the electricity supply industry the previous April (1948), and took the control of the provision of electricity away from the local authority.

Above and Right: *Sorting out the new electric lights on Royal Parade.*

The general consequence of all this competition was that post-war Plymouth was much more effectively lit than it had ever been before. Mutley Plain, the main shopping thoroughfare for the city in the late-forties, was the first to get the full fluorescent treatment, in 1950, and it wasn't long before the Plymouth Joint Road Safety Committee decided to recommend to the Street Lighting Committee that all pedestrian-crossings in Royal Parade should be floodlit. This followed an earlier suggestion by Mr HP Twyford that flashing signs before pedestrian crossings did not show up pedestrians on the black stripes of zebra crossing. The floodlighting was to be similar to that used on Mutley Plain before the installation of fluorescent lighting.

All this helped make the streets much safer at night, but there were still fines in place for any motorist caught parking their cars at night without front or rear lights. The fine was a fairly hefty one too: one pound for cars and £1.10.0d (£1.50) for lorries.

In Plymouth, the Chief Constable was relatively relaxed about the matter when a car was parked in a brightly lit street, but in Saltash (and Cornwall generally) it remained an issue throughout the fifties and in 1959 the Chamber of Commerce appealed to the Chief Constable of Cornwall to allow parking without lights in the 'fluorescent-lit shopping centre' of the town.

Opposite page: Mutley Plain becomes the first major city thoroughfare to be illuminated by flourescent lighting. Above: Armada Way. Top right: Milehouse (note the illuminated clock on the bus station building). Bottom: Norwich Union.

WORK AND HOME LIFE

One inevitable consequence of the ever-increasing provision of electric lighting and the ever-growing appetite for and availability of electrical goods, was the need to provide more and more electricity to power these developments. Less than twelve months after the war had ended the Central Electricity Generating Board tasked Plymouth with the job of extending its facilities: however, following the Nationalisation of the Industry, two years later, the project came under the control of the British Electricity Authority. That same year preliminary site-clearance work was undertaken for the new (Plymouth 'B') power station, a much larger and more powerful concern than Plymouth 'A' alongside it.

As if to underline the importance of the original Plymouth operation the City's Electrical Engineer, Harold Midgeley, was appointed deputy chairman of the new South Western Electricity Board and Alderman HJ (Heber) Perry became chairman of the South Western Electricity Consultative Council, a body set up to provide the board with the perspective and interests of electricity consumers.

Initially planned as a coal-fired station, the first phase of Plymouth 'B' was completed in 1953 and the second phase in 1959, at which time it was converted to an oil-fired facility.

Paraffin oil (artificially coloured so that companies could promote their own brand) was another popular source of fuel for domestic heaters, with Esso Blue (from Standard Oil - hence S-O), Aladdin Pink, and White May (from BP) being the market leaders with Regent's Super Green some way behind them.

Left: Work began on clearing the site for Plymouth's new power station in 1948 and phase one (above right) was completed in 1953.

Put yourself in this picture. The quiet refined luxury of this room can be yours.

Many more elegant Suites such as this, as well as Carpets and other charming accessories, can all be seen in our Showrooms.

Charles
HARDING
(PLYMOUTH) LTD.
of
mutley plain

ADVERTISEMENTS 239

G-PLAN FURNITURE

Waxed Oak Furniture of pleasing design which can be used as individual pieces or as a normal Bedroom Suite

Each article is separately priced and extra pieces can be purchased as required

Call at our Showrooms on Mutley Plain and see the wide range of Furniture displayed

CHARLES HARDING
of Mutley Plain

Not everything was nationally, or internationally branded, however, and there were still many manufacturing operations dotted around the city.

Charles Harding not only had one of the largest furniture stores in the area, they also had a sizeable factory where they made, repaired and generally upholstered a wide variety of items for the modern home. Clearly though there were restrictions immediately after the war.

Following the widespread bombing of Britain in 1941 and the inevitable shortage of timber there was an urgent need to address the wood issue and in 1942 the Utility Furniture Advisory Committee was set up. Shortly afterwards, the supply of all new furniture was rationed, only those who had been bombed out of house and home or newly weds were eligible.

Essentially the idea was to cut down on wastage and an eminent team of experts and designers was put together to advise on how best to get the most out of existing supplies.

On 1 January 1943 the Committee published their first Utility Furniture Catalogue and supplied it to some 700 firms around the country.

'Everything had to be marked with a stamp, you couldn't make anything that wasn't in the catalogue.' (Sid Oliver chair-frame maker)

The stamp was the same as the one that had been produced earlier for the Utility Clothing scheme and comprised two capital 'C's and the number 41, the whole standing for 'Civilian Clothing 1941'. Designed by Reginald Shipp it was quickly and not very surprisingly nicknamed 'The Cheeses' (see left).

Later in 1943 the Committee was restyled as the Design Panel and just after the end of the war, in 1946, they oversaw a major exhibition – Britain Can Make It – at which time they launched three new ranges of furniture: Cotswold, Chiltern and Cockaigne.

Despite the Panel's best efforts to produce attractive and stylish furniture the great British public craved more colourful and extravagant products and although a new 'Diversified' range was introduced in 1948, public support for the initiative was dwindling and at the end of the year the Panel was wound down, although many manufacturers persevered with the designs until the scheme was officially ended in 1952.

Inside Charles Harding's Mutley workshop.

UTILITY FURNITURE

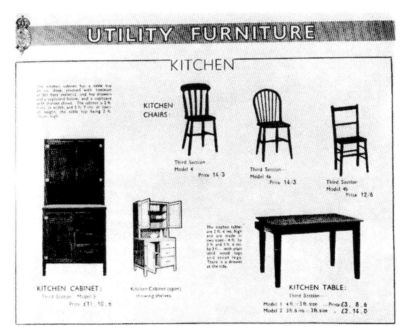

KITCHEN

KITCHEN CHAIRS:

Third Section—
Model 4
Price 14/3

Third Section—
Model 4a
Price 14/3

Third Section
Model 4b
Price 12/6

KITCHEN CABINET:
Third Section — Model 5
Price £11.10.6

Kitchen Cabinet (open)
showing shelves.

KITCHEN TABLE:
Third Section
Model 1 4ft × 3ft size   Price £3.8.6
Model 2 3ft.6ins × 3ft.size   £2.14.0

Locally, Frank Northmore, off Wesley Avenue, had one of the firms that supplied Charles Harding with chair frames as well as some of the other upholsterers in the area: Newberry's, Rundle Rogers & Brook, and Jubilee Floating Springs, in Union Street, run by Bob Baker. There were one or two other manufacturers around the area – Clatworthy in Clare Place and Kimber in Stillman Street - but most furniture dealers were dedicated retailers, Hilda M Haddon, in Cobourg Street and Ebrington Street had one of the better-known businesses.

Ken Hopkin's Co-operative Removal van on Dartmoor c.1954.

The austerity measures that afflicted the furniture world had already made an impact on the wartime textile and clothing industry; women were encouraged to 'Make Do And Mend', while Mrs Sew And Sew actively encouraged everyone to recycle material whenever possible. While most households had someone proficient at darning socks, turning collars or knitting anything from a swimsuit to a woolly hat or cardigan, shoe repairing tended to be a specialist job and one that Fred Parsons (a veteran of Scott's Polar Expedition) made into a thriving business.

With a neat marketing ploy of putting postcards through doors offering prompt collection and return delivery, and claiming the City's Quickest and Best Shoe Repair Service, Parson's distinctive fleet of maroon and cream vans were a common site around the town.

'We have no Medals or Diplomas. The large amount of time spent to produce exhibition work is of no benefit to the Customer. We spend our time Supervising the Employees producing the Commercial Job, i.e. YOUR WORK. May we serve you?'

And then there was their invisible mending slogan: 'You can't see what you pay for!'

There were plenty of other boot and shoe repairers around the city,

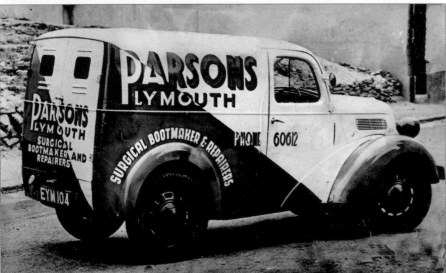

This page, top left: *Fred Parsons and the workers to whom he sold his business.* Bottom left: *A Parsons' van signwritten by Hastings Street neighbour Colour-Ads.* Right: *the factory in Hastings Street.* Opposite page: *Edna Furze and the girls of Dent's glove factory in Alvington Street, Cattedown: 'We made gloves – fabric and leather – mittens, slippers, coats (sheepskin and leather).'*

The HOUSE of Moons

PIANOS
FURNITURE
RADIO AND
MUSICAL
INSTRUMENTS

ALSO

GRAMOPHONES
AND RECORDS

and plenty of other firms that not only sold things, but could fix them too.

Moons were the main music and musical instrument people in town – there was also Yardley's, Parker & Smith, and Frank Harris.

Bombed out of their George Street premises in 1941, the long-established company with five other branches across Devon and Cornwall, spread themselves across three locations – Ebrington Street, St Andrew Street and Queen Anne Terrace – while they waited for position in New George Street.

As it was, they moved into the new double-fronted premises, in October 1956, just three years ahead of their 150th anniversary.

Valued as these smaller manufacturing bases were they were never going to be enough to support the labour market in the post-war period. With unemployment running at twice the national average - in spite of the massive amount of building work going on around the city – the picture in Plymouth was particularly bleak. Already one of the larger factories, Reckitt & Colman Ltd. (manufacturers of starch, blue, and black lead), had decided not to re-establish their local offshoot after being bombed out of Sutton Road. Opting instead to concentrate on their headquarters in Hull (as Reckitt Benckiser, today it is the world's largest producer of household goods, among them Dettol, Strepsils, Veet, Vanish, Air Wick, and Durex – with operations in over 60 countries around the world).

With the number of men employed in the Dockyard bound to fall with the advent of peace, the Chamber of Commerce were one of the many voices urging Central Government to help out.

In 1946 the Board of Trade sent three firms to the area, all looking for favourable terms to start up new manufacturing bases.

First to arrive were the international lubrication and filtration giants, Tecalemit who started to establish themselves here in 1947. They could so easily have chosen somewhere in Wales or Scotland, but Plymouth City Council was very keen to lure the firm here and 'laid out a welcome mat over 62 acres at Marsh Mills'.

Above: Harry Bolt and Ted Brooks in Moon's workshop on North Hill.

Above and opposite page: Tecalemit at Marsh Mills.

By Christmas 1951 the first phase of the factory with its soft-orange Taunton brick walls and honey-toned, Ham hill coping-stone, was complete, although it would be another couple of years before the massive canteen (soon a popular dance venue) would be built.

Major suppliers to the motor industry, the enterprise locally was eventually more like five factories in one and quickly became the biggest factory of the largest company in that field, in the world, employing thousands of men and hundreds of women.

Bush Radio followed hot on the heels of Tecalemit, their new factory being opened by Lady Astor on the Ernesettle estate at the end of June 1949.

In no time at all these two factories each had the largest pool of civilian employees – as opposed to civil servants – in the city, with around two and half thousand workers apiece.

Remarkably, the Rank-Bush-Murphy outfit at Ernesettle was the largest television production unit in Europe (although ironically, for the first few years here, the sets were of no use locally, as there was no reception in this part of the world).

Next to arrive were dress manufacturers Berketex, who soon had 1,000 employees on their books in Honicknowle.

Opposite page: *The Tecalemit toolroom.* Above left: *A moblie exhibition stand at Hyde Park School.*
Top right: *Home time and hundreds leave the site in just a few minutes.* Bottom: *Factory work.*

July 1951 inside the finance office of Marks & Spencer – note the one pound notes in bundles on the desk, and the heavily pregnant young lady in the corner.

While the new factories facilitated life on the new estates, the bulk of the civilian workforce was still focussed around the city centre, out as far as Cattedown to the east, Stonehouse to the West and Mutley Plain to the north.

Even throughout the lengthy rebuilding process this was where the main action was:

The main organs of local information dissemination – the newspapers, were all based here. The massive presses of the *Western Morning News* and *Western Evening Herald* which had run with barely an interruption throughout the war, were here at the back of the former Frankfort Street premises, Leicester Harmsworth House, which had opened on 1 December 1938. This was the home of the *Football Herald* too, while the *Western Independent* and *South Devon Times* operated out of Alton Terrace, the *Plymouth Weekly Gazette*, from premises on Mutley Plain (where the *Herald* and *Morning News* also had an office), and the *Daily Mirror* had an editorial outpost in St Andrew Street.

Typesetters, typists and copytakers ruled the roost and every journalist worth their salt could do shorthand, as could most secretarial staff. In accounts departments mental arithmetic skills were an absolute essential, although increasingly adding machines and card-punch machines were finding favour with those at the cutting edge of the new technology.

'In January 1949, having left school at the age of 15, I joined the Accounts Department of SWEB as a punch operator, earning the grand sum of £2.0s.8d per week. This department was then located in Armada Street, Plymouth. All the punch machines were of the Hollerith hand punch type.

'From the Hollerith we "graduated" to the sorting, collating and printing machines: these produced the quarterly electricity accounts for this area. Those of us using these machines were issued with thick, blue overalls, but not, unfortunately, ear plugs, as the noise of these larger machines was deafening.'
(Fran Michael – née Meese)

Top right: Girls operating sorting, collating and printing machines in the SWEB office. Bottom: Girls in the general office of Marks & Spencer, 1955, note the adding machine and the Guinness Clock outside the window.

Marty Fenton, Reggie Giles and Bob Borrows on their 250cc BSA bikes outside the Telegram Boy's hut in front of the GPO Telephone Exchange building off Ebrington Street.
Opposite page clockwise: The sort of telegram that nobody wanted. Ken Hill with the manager's car to his left. Looking out towards Ebrington Street and Moon's Music Store.

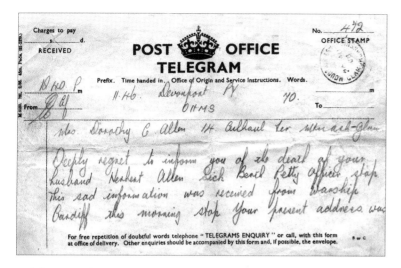

POST OFFICE TELEGRAM

Charges to pay RECEIVED
No. 472 OFFICE STAMP

Prefix. Time handed in. Office of Origin and Service Instructions. Words.

11.46 Devonport PV 70

OHMS

Mrs. Dorothy C Allen 14 Aulhaul ter Mevagh-Glen

Deeply regret to inform you of the death of your husband Herbert Allen Sick Berth Petty Officer stop this sad information was received from warship Cardiff this morning stop Your present address was

For free repetition of doubtful words telephone "TELEGRAMS ENQUIRY" or call, with this form at office of delivery. Other enquiries should be accompanied by this form and, if possible, the envelope.

While young females tended to dominate the office environment, one field that was the exclusive domain of the young male was the Post Office Telegram.

Originally on pushbikes, they were replaced soon after the war by BSA 250cc side-valve machines, until they were deemed to be too fast for the job, or at least for the young men riding them, and the engine size was halved and BSA Bantams replaced the bigger bikes.

'They were 1946 models, rigid framed at first, with girder forks, but soon evolving into sprung frame models with telescopic forks.

'The motorcycles were returned to the GPO garage in Central Park Avenue each night for garaging, servicing etc., and collected from there each morning for telegram delivery from the hut off Ebrington Street.' (Dag Jennings, GPO Messenger 1946-47)

Like the bikes, the headgear also went through a transformation process:

'That big hut was a horrible design. One bit of wind and it was off!'

As for the work itself: 'It wasn't a bad job; we used to deliver a lot of flowers in those days, especially Jersey ones – mainly to older ladies. We'd have quite a bit of kosher meat to take around on Thursday, and post bets to bookies.' (Ken Hill, who like many served as a messenger boy for three years before starting work as a junior

For a lot of local lads however an apprenticeship, combined with a bit of National Service, was a common, post-school route:

'I started my apprenticeship in the joiner's shop of the Plymouth Co-operative Society in 1948, mainly jobbing work at first, working on various Co-operative Stores and Farms. Then I was put on the first phase of what would become Co-operative House (Derry's) on Royal Parade.

'Soon after I completed my apprenticeship however I was drafted into the Army, for National Service, in 1954, after which I went back into the Co-op to work on the second phase of the new Co-operative store, until it was completed at the beginning of the sixties.

'Not long after that I went into the Joiners' Shop in Devonport Dockyard, before later transferring to the Works Department of Her Majesty's Prison Dartmoor, at Princetown.' (Ian Bickle)

The Dockyard and the building trade certainly provided the largest employment prospects to young men in the immediate post-war period, but there were quite a few other industries that operated around and about, with Willoughby's Ship Repairers, Boilermakers, and Fitters one of the more significant others operating out of Millbay, with Blight and White, Steel Fabricators and Constructors, out at Prince Rock, another.

BLIGHT & WHITE, LTD.

MANUFACTURE ALL TYPES OF
STEEL-FRAMED
BUILDINGS

IN THEIR MODERN FACTORY AT
PRINCE ROCK
PLYMOUTH

*

MAY WE DESIGN AND QUOTE FOR YOUR
REQUIREMENTS?

*

Phone: 3437/9   Grams: Steelwork, Plymouth

Blight and White supplied much of the framework for modern Plymouth, however, not withstanding the various employment opportunities around the city, there was still more unemployment here than in most parts of the country, and people generally had to be careful with their money, however such is not to say that they couldn't afford the occasional night out.

Top: *Ian Bickle and fellow apprentice Charlie Avery, working on the first phase of the then new Co-operative House, on Royal Parade, with St Andrew's and the Guildhall, not yet restored in the background.* Bottom: *Harold Bouncer outside the weighbridge at the Coal Wharf on Sutton Harbour, with colleagues including Sam Coniam, Jimmy Hodge.*

Some of the men who helped rebuild Plymouth after the war, prior to the removal of the shell of the Municipal Building. Reg Pollard second from left, kneeling.

The Theatre Royal in 1955 with a small queue there for Seven Brides for Seven Brothers, note the corner premises originally home of Fullers Restaurant.

THAT'S ENTERTAINMENT

Pre-dating the post-war Plymouth City Centre fashion for Portland Stone, the Theatre Royal (as it was still being referred to in 1955) was one of 45 cinemas around the country designed by William Riddle Glenn for the Associated British Cinema (ABC) chain – it was a building evidently much admired by Patrick Abercrombie. Curiously enough, it was never intended that the Royal should have stood on its own. After the demolition of the original Theatre Royal, it was always the plan to have a new hotel alongside the new cinema. In the event, the old Theatre Royal came down in 1937, and the new one went up on its site in 1938 – it's façade saw-toothed on the eastern side ready for its new neighbour. However, the old Royal Hotel stayed where it was … until 1941 when the building was devastated in the Blitz and here we see, alongside the cinema, the temporary NAAFI club housed in a thinly disguised collection of Nissen Huts.

Inside the cinema itself was a wonderful Compton organ, played from 1938 and throughout the forties and fifties by local lad Dudley Savage. The cinema's spacious auditorium could house over 2,400 (1,564 in the stalls and 840 in the circle) and in the late fifties it was increasingly pressed into service as a live venue.

1955 and note saw-toothed side of the Theatre facade.

223

Although a long way from Hollywood, Plymouth did occasionally have visits from American movie stars, not just passing through Millbay Station en route for London, or opening shops in the new City Centre, but also promoting their latest films at the City's cinemas. Dolores Gray was among them, she appeared in two of MGM's big films of 1955, 'Kismet' and 'It's Always Fairweather', having lent her voice to Marylin Monroe's vocal role on the soundtrack of the previous year's 'There's No Business Like Show Business'.

Dolores's Plymouth visit saw her welcomed to the Plaza Cinema in Exeter Street, by the manager Mr Holman.

Other Plymouth Cinemas open throughout the forties and fifties included the State in St Budeaux, the Forum in Devonport, the Ford Palladium, in St Levan Road, the Belgrave, off Mutley Plain, the Gaumont in Union Street and the Odeon, formerly of Frankfort Street and then New George Street.

All of them had been built before the war and all benefitted indirectly from the demise of a number of their competitors during the war: notably the Cinedrome and the Palladium in Ebrington Street, the Criterion in Cornwall Street, plus a handful of Union Street cinemas – the Embassy, the Grand, the Lyric and the Savoy. A couple of them, like the Grand, had formerly been theatres, as had the Hippodrome in Devonport, which, like Devonport's Tivoli and Electric, was also lost in the Blitz.

Above: *The Gaumont 1949, showing Dick Barton Special Agent and the Bandit of Sherwood Forest.*
Top right: *Staff member Lilian Pitts, receives a presentation from Dolores Gray at the Plaza.*

Of the main Plymouth cinemas to have survived the war, all but one – the Odeon – were to survive the post-war redevelopment, and even that made it into the sixties.

Notwithstanding that, however, all these big screen entertainment venues started to struggle in the face of a common enemy – the small screen that was increasingly finding its way into almost every house in the country – the television.

And small screens they were too, most sets (typically rented Rediffusion sets or Bush – made locally – or Decca, Pye or GEC) were around nine inches across and black and white only with, up until 1955, when commercial television was launched, only the one channel available – from the BBC.

Even then, prior to the advent of ITV, viewing options were far from continuous, programming ending before midnight each night (the National Anthem signalling close down) and a so-called Toddler's Truce between 6pm and 7pm when no programmes were shown (so that young children could be put to bed).

Above: *The Odeon in 1953*. Right: *Seen in context, at the end of King Street..*

Programmes and posters from the Palace Theatre. Middle top: Francine Baker's grandfather, a doorman at the Palace.

Whatever the comparative limitations of the new medium, its impact on all other sources of entertainment was enormous as people became less and less likely to venture out of their homes once broadcasting had begun. The cinema suffered, as did all sports and other cultural diversions, live and otherwise.

Among those particularly badly hit was the Palace of Varieties in Union Street, where it became increasingly important, ironically enough, for any act to have had some sort of presence on radio, television or at the cinema in order to be able to pull in a crowd. But there was another problem too for, as the post-war drive to rehouse the cramped and crowded population of Plymouth took effect, so the inner-city population fell away. Around the Palace Theatre there had been a lot of high-density housing before the war, now the Plan suggested that the figure of '100 persons per acre would be reduced to about 56 persons per acre, which might be taken as the average residential density proposed for central Plymouth.'

Amongst other things this meant clearing Chapel Street, George Street, East Street, Hobart Street, Brownlow Street, Market Street, St Mary Street, Millbay Terrace and parts of Emma Place. Clearly it also meant a substantial movement of people. 'The total pre-war population of the area of the scheme as a whole was 23,112 persons, of which 8,352 are re-housed in the redevelopment scheme, leaving 14,760 persons to be accommodated in the other areas, 6,324 of these being displaced by the zoning of the southern section (below Union Street) for industry. This 65 per cent of the population is a considerable measure of decentralisation.' (Plan for Plymouth)

Before the war whenever there had been entertainment in Union Street there had been an audience near at hand, now 'the garish atmosphere of Union Street with its milling crowds had gone. So had the cosmopolitan night life of the city centre with its cosy, friendly atmosphere where one could be sure of meeting at least one acquaintance at Genoni's restaurant or in one of the long bars of the pubs, much to the regret of older Plymothians who retained faithful memories of the old city with its higgledy-piggledy streets. For whatever its geographical drawbacks, the old Plymouth had a soul and a character of its own and comprised a community that had lived closely together for generations. Industry, citizens and administration were interwoven, all within easy reach, with the result that entertainment was near or at hand whenever required.' (Harvey Crane, Playbill)

After succeeding her husband and running the Palace throughout the war, Mrs Hoyle sold up in 1945. Gerard Heath headed the syndicate that took over, but he struggled. Meanwhile, plans to reopen the damaged Grand Theatre were postponed again and again. In common with other theatres up and down the country the Palace experimented with shows that were too daring or risque for radio or television: 'Fanny Get Your Fun' starring the glamorous Julie, or 'Funny Face' with Alec Pleon. But it wasn't enough and in 1956 the Palace closed.

Top: A photo signed by Stan Laurel and Oliver Hardy for Palace Theatre lighting man Stan Evans. Below: Their last programme.

Throughout this period, however, there were times when the Palace thrived, notably at Christmas and panto time, the clowning Charlie Cairoli was a favourite and appeared in the 1953 production of 'Little Miss Muffet', while Gracie Field's younger brother Tommy starred the following year as Buttons in Emile Littler's 'Cinderella'. Tickets ranged from 2/- to 9/6d (10p to 49p).

It was Plymouth's festive season with television: '*Between 60 and 80 television licenses are being bought daily in the Plymouth area. Nearly 2,000 licenses have been taken out – almost 500 of them since the end of November. A Plymouth television dealer said on Saturday, the day after the opening of the service from North Hessary Tor, that television business was now booming in the city.*'

Another dealer warned potential customers that: '*A television set is something like a car in that you have to familiarise yourself with it to get the best results. The only trouble likely to arise in a new set could be caused by 'turning the wrong knob'. What we have usually found is that after turning the wrong knob, the owner, in an attempt to rectify matters, turns other knobs and gets deeper in the mire until he has to send for the engineers. When something goes wrong it was usually the fault of a customer who is known in the trade as a "twiddler".*' (*Western Evening Herald*; December 1954)

The vast majority of the population, however, were without a television and so for the time being the Palace, the delightful little Globe Theatre in the Royal Marine Barracks, the marvellous Little Theatre on the Barbican and even the halls and canteens of Berketex and Tecalemit, were able to successfully stage some fine amateur dramatic productions courtesy of companies like the Tamaritans, Carmenians, Western College Players and the Plympton Wranglers.

Top: *1954 Tommy Fields as Buttons*. Bottom: *1953 Charlie Cairoli in Little Miss Muffet*. Right: *Babs Owen rehearses some dancers*. Far Right: *Fairies from King Oggie of Guz*.

Clockwise from top left: 1952 'Treasure Hunt' at the Globe Theatre, produced by Vera Sparkes
l-r: Norman May, Joan Warne, Valerie Power, Amy Everett, David Bishop (later Plymouth's Coroner),
David King, Barbara Vercoe, Frank Horton, Cyril Penrose, Anne Christie, Sandy Ewing (local
GP) and Wendy Ayres. 1955 poster for 'King Oggie of Guz', produced by Harvey Crane and
performed by the Dockyard Players in the Globe. Inside the Globe. Plympton Wranglers 1951
production of 'Babes in the Wood' - a young David Owen, third from left front row.

The big new factory canteens – at Bush, Berketex and Tecalemit – were also pressed into service as dance halls as were one or two of the new school halls, notably Honicknowle, and various village halls around and about. In the city itself, Exmouth Hall at Devonport, the Embassy at Milehouse and the Mutley Assembly Rooms were very popular, while among the pre-war survivors in the centre the Corn Exchange, the Park Ballroom and the Lecture Hall of the Guildhall competed with the big hotels – the Duke of Cornwall and the Continental – as the most popular venues.

Many of these events were alcohol free, and neighbouring pubs would often do a good trade before the proceedings started and during the interval - the Chimes in Catherine Street was popular with dancers at the Lecture Hall.

Typically evenings started around 8pm and there was unlikely to be any admission after 10pm with 11pm the usual finish time and the cost, somewhere in the region of a couple of bob (2/- or 10p).

Soon after the war the local Musicians Union instigated a major annual dance, and in 1953 the ball that was held at the Tecalemit Factory attracted over 1,000 dances and was reckoned to be the biggest event of its kind west of Bristol since the cessation of hostilities.

The bands taking part in what amounted to six hours of non-stop playing were: Harry Brown and his band, Ted Coleman and his Waldorf orchestra, George Day and his string orchestra for old-time, Frank Fuge and his orchestra, Bob Janes and his Group, Plymouth Swing Band, Jock West and his Rumba Band, Mutley Dance Orchestra and Les Watts and his Band. The Chairman was Mr E Redmore and the MCs were Messrs Frank Fuge, Douglas Attrill, and Howard Rowland.

Big band swing was still the thing and among the other main bands around at the time were Art Danes, Art Thomas, Les Colmer, Jack Johns, Jimmy Warren, Lou Gerry, Lionel Patten, Edgar Denley and Fred Cleaver.

As well as being, albeit unintentionally, a quasi training ground for local dance band musicians, the Royal Marine Band (Plymouth) was ever a major attraction and always pulled a big crowd wherever they played; the Hoe being one of their regular haunts.

Top: *At the Continental Hotel with Jack Johns; Reg Ashley on bass, Alf Potter, piano, Chris Ramsey, first alto, Charlie Coombes, second alto, and Les Brown and Jimmy trumpet.* Bottom: *On the roof of the Paramount Ballroom circa 1946 with Les Stoneman, trombone, Doug Mutton, Bill Jackson and Jimmy Warren, trumpet, Reg Arnold, lead alto, and Herbie Mills, drums.*

Clockwise from the top left: Art Danes; Terry Spetigue, drums, George Ireland, bass, Ron Gracie/Bert Kingwell, seated, piano, saxes left to right, Ian James, Jack Clark, Jock Craig, Tony McQuarry and Ralph Babbage, with Jimmy Warren on trumpet, far right at Tecalemit; Ted Coleman; Sheila Pester and Brian Bishop singing with Ted Coleman's Band at a Tecalemit Ball; Art Thomas; Les Watts Band.

. . . but he never misses a good programme with

RADIO TIMES

EVERY FRIDAY

Radio Times advert. Uncle Mac - Derek McCulloch. Bottom: BBC studio, Seymour Road, 1955.

In those pre-television days if you wanted other than home-made music and entertainment without stepping outside your front door, you were almost certainly reliant on the gramophone or the wireless and one can't help but wonder if the BBC's decision to launch a new serial, based around a fictional family in a fictional West Country town – Dimstock, said to be modelled on Plymstock – in 1948, was in part driven by the fact that Aunty was uncomfortable at her lack of reach down here.

Although the radio licence fee (at one pound) was only half that of the combined radio and television fee it was, nevertheless, double what it had been during wartime and many were concerned at the increase when it was announced in the summer of 1946.

Thus it was that the locally generated 'At The Luscombes' first hit Home Service on 24 September 1948 and predated the 'Archers' by over two years. Michael Holloway was the story-teller and it wasn't long before the nation was familiar with Mr and Mrs Luscombe's pet expressions. With swearing absolutely out of the question on daytime broadcasting, indeed any broadcasting, an exasperated Pop Luscombe could regularly be heard to exclaim: *'Cor lummie Charlie'* or *'Dash my buttons!'* while Mrs L (Flo) would often conclude a conversation with *'Well, you know best'* when clearly she didn't think so!

A more obvious local link was with Derek McCulloch the radio voice of Larry the Lamb and the presenter of the popular Saturday morning children's request programme Children's Favourites. Best known as Uncle Mac, Derek was born in Plymouth in 1897 and apart from his wireless work as a producer and a presenter, the Great War veteran (he lost an eye at the Battle of the Somme) was also something of an author lending his name to six Ladybird books, including 'Beside the Sea' with Uncle Mac, and penning two children's adventure stories - 'Cornish Mystery' and 'Cornish Adventure'.

Other output included locally produced documentaries, football results and a music-request programme.

On one notable occasion the presenter, who had a reputation for enjoying a drink, went to play a 78-rpm recording by Frederick Harvey only to accidentally break the disc just before transmission. Ever resourceful he rang Frederick Harvey, who lived close to the BBC in Mannamead and persuaded him to come into the studio and sing the song live - there was a piano in the studio!

In November 1949 Frederick Harvey had sung at the Royal Performance, it had been a musical tribute to HMS *Amethyst* with the Royal Marine Band under the baton of Major Vivian Dunn.

Born in Plymouth and educated at Plymouth College, young Frederick had been a chorister at St Andrew's Church and for some seventeen years before becoming a professional singer had enjoyed the vocal training given him by the celebrated Dr Harold Moreton, St Andrew's long-standing organist and choirmaster.

Frederick was a great favourite on the BBC in the early days of the wireless. He had made his first recordings, aged just 21, back in 1929, having won a prize in a singing competition sponsored by Columbia Records.

During the war, serving as a lieutenant in the RNVR, he recorded a number of sessions with the Portsmouth Royal Marine Band and after the war he sang in all the major concert venues across the country and was a regular on the BBC's 'Friday Night Is Music Night' and 'Grand Hotel'.

"My father bought this state of the art tape recorder – it cost about £1,000 back in the late 1940s and would use it for practice and to record broadcasts. He would ring my mother in the fifteen-minute break they had in the middle of doing 'Friday Night is Music Night', live in London, and ask her how it was sounding and she would tell him to back off the microphone or stand closer or just give it a bit more umph. When he came home on the train and had got back to the house he'd sit and analyse the recording.' (John Harvey)

One of the quirkier events locally during this time was the visit to the Corn Exchange of James Strickleton, better known as Syncopating Sandy the marathon piano player.

Sandy toured the country with his bizarre endurance act and would always attempt to create a new world record for playing the piano non-stop, taking his meals at the keyboard, with his assistant pulling a curtain across so that he could play 'Lady of Spain' one-handed (allegedly) when nature called! Audiences could come and go as they pleased. His own record appears to have been just over 193 hours and it is said that on one occasion, in Keighly, he smoked over 600 cigarettes in a 133-hour stint.

ROYAL FESTIVAL HALL
GENERAL MANAGER: T. E. BEAN

The LCC and the BBC Light Programme present

the LIGHT PROGRAMME
music festival of 1955

PROGRAMME PRICE ONE SHILLING

Top: Frederick Harvey and a programme from one of the many events at which he sang. Bottom: Syncopating Sandy, the marathon piano player, at the Corn Exchange - sponsore by Mason's evidently!

233

Among the other entertainments available locally of course was the fairground and here too peace brought dividends:

'The fairground enjoyed a bumper year in 1945 and orders for new rides flooded in to suppliers at home and abroad. Whiteleggs started their season at Camel's head, in Plymouth, a ground that had been used before the war.' (Guy Belshaw *T Whitelegg & Sons, Cavalcade of Shows*)

In 1946 Whiteleggs unveiled their first new post-war ride, the American-built Eli Bridge Big Wheel, it proved to be an instant hit and was the first big wheel to be permanently based in the far west.

After purchasing a number of new vehicles to haul their fair from town to town, and a new set of generators, one of which was called the City of Plymouth, Whiteleggs acquired a few other new attractions, including a set of gallopers from George Whittle, whose name continued to grace the roundabout for some years.

In 1949 a new set of dodgems came down to the fair, delivered by train and in 1950 Tom Whitelegg commissioned a boxing booth. In the event it was built by Hurley's the Plymouth boat builders and decorated by the Colour-Ads proprietor Frank Cobbledick.

'Boxing booths had a strong tradition in the west, and other presenters included Alf Wright and Jack and Alice Gratton, and their son, Johnny 'One Round' Gratton.' (Guy Belshaw)

Above: Whitelegg's Chair-o-planes on Quay Road. Right: Mickey Kiely's West of England Boxing Academy outside the Dolphin on the Barbican.

Central Park, Mutton Cove, Colebrook, the Barbican, Elphinstone, and the Hoe, were all regular venues for the fair and Anderton and Rowland were the other great families of Showmen who were bringing their entertainments to the city.

The freshly demobbed George De Vey took charge of the A&R concern in the spring of 1946. Incidentally, the fact that the De Veys 'had fought for "King and Country" in the war, at the expense of their business, whilst Whiteleggs had continued to travel and done very well out of it' engendered, at the time, an additional degree of resentment between the two rival showground enterprises.

Another of the city's favourite visitors to Central Park was the Chipperfield Circus. The firm had originated in Falmouth over 200 years earlier and local connections were cemented when, well into the twentieth century, the future Administrative Director of the Circus, Richard Chipperfield, maried a Devonport girl.

Above: *Dodgems, forties-style.* Top right: *The Fairground comes to town.* Bottom, middle and right: *The Circus comes to town, Billy Smart's troupe parading through the City Centre.*

Dodgems, Chair-o-Planes, Ferris Wheels, and Waltzers weren't the only incentives for people to venture out for a bit of excitement, there were plenty of other outdoor entertainments, often, like the local Carnival and Gala, part sponsored or at least supported by one of the fairground operators. Among such events were the annual events staged at Colebrook (Plympton) and Oreston (Plymstock).

Plympton and Plymstock on the other side of the Plym from Plymouth, were entirely separate from the big city, but not from each other and it was within the gift of Plympton Rural District Council to grant permission for the organisers of the Oreston and District Carnival to use the playing field at Oreston for their annual jolly. Furthermore, in 1948 at least, the President of the Plympton Rural District Council, Captain George Farrer Viner, was on hand to perform the ceremonial duties, foremost among which was the all-important crowning of the Carnival Queen.

The event, like the celebrated Honicknowle Week, which was also revived after the war, stretched over six days and included a great range of attractions and activities, not all of which took place in the field, as among the land and waterside events there was sailing, rowing, swimming and diving. With live music courtesy of the Plymouth Silver Band, the carnival was a truly memorable occasion.

1949 Oreston and District Carnival poster. Right: August 1948 - Captain Viner kisses the gloved hand of Oreston Carnival Queen June Callan.

Tense action shot from the 1949 Oreston Carnival egg and spoon race.

Coxside pram race c.1950

Not every community was fortunate enough to have a large open field on their doorstep however, but that was never a good reason not to have a bit of fun. The travelling fairground was always a big attraction on the Barbican, but that didn't mean that the local folk couldn't create their own entertainment and the Annual Sutton Harbour Regatta provided an opportunity to dress up, be silly and have a laugh.

Barrel-racing, pram-racing, sack-racing, the greasy-pole challenge, mudwrestling, tug-o-war and apple-bobbing were all part of the regular rituals, along with the great trawler race itself. Dozens of fishing-boats, awash with coloured flags and bunting, clamoured to get out of Sutton Harbour before setting off on a mad dash around the Sound and back.

Residents on both sides of the Harbour, on the Barbican and in Coxside would join in the fun, with the washed-down fish market traditionally playing host to a hoedown on the Saturday night.

The Hoe itself, of course, was the more formal venue for Civic Events and it was gaily lit for the Festival of Britain celebrations across the summer of 1951, the King formally opening the event on 3 May in London.

Above: *1950s Barbican Regatta, on the left is the landlord, in fancy dress, of the Crown & Anchor, to the right of the tug of war team is Mabel Easton. Inset: Plymouth Hoe lights up for the Festival of Britain.*

239

Main photo: *Life-size chess at West Hoe.* Inset top: *Elizabethan bowls.* Bottom right: *Marching towards the Citadel.*

Little could anyone have anticipated then that nine months later the King would have passed on at the age of 56 and his eldest daughter, twenty-five-year-old Elizabeth Alexandra Mary would have succeeded him.

With no immediate plans for a coronation, it gave everyone plenty of time to prepare, and for those in an area with reception, an opportunity to think about renting or buying a television set. This was the first Coronation to be watched live on the small screen and across the country the number of TV licences doubled to over three million, while it was estimated that more than 20 million British citizens watched television for the first time ever, most in the homes of friends, family or neighbours (in America incidentally it was estimated that almost 100 million people witnessed the event via recorded transmissions).

Plymouth, still on the periphery as far as television was concerned, decided to celebrate the occasion with two weeks of events either side of Coronation Day. These were primarily based in and around the Hoe but there were also concerts in Devonport Park, Raglan Barracks and Central Park. They featured the City of Plymouth Light Orchestra, the Plymouth Silver Band and the Royal Marine Band - as well as dances in the Corn Exchange, The Lecture Hall, and Devonport Guildhall.

On the Friday and Saturday before the big day, the Lord Mayor, Alderman Sir Clifford Tozer, and the City Council entertained 2,500 'Aged Persons to a Tea and Entertainment in the Drill Shed of the Royal Naval Barracks'.

Meanwhile, on the big day itself, the proceedings started at 10am with a Naval, Military, Air Force and Civilian Coronation Parade Service on the Hoe Promenade, followed by a Royal Salute from the guns of the Royal Citadel, Eastern King's, Devonport Naval Barracks, and the those of Her Majesty's ships that were in the harbour.

In the afternoon there was a bowling match in Elizabethan costume just below the war memorial, a children's talent contest in a large marquee alongside and, on the West Hoe Recreation Ground, a live chess display presented by the Plymouth Chess Club.

On the Promenade afternoon square dancing was followed by alfresco dancing with Ted Coleman's Orchestra, followed by selections from the Royal Marine Band. At 8.55pm the Prime Minister's broadcast was relayed via loudspeakers, followed by a broadcast from the Queen herself at 9pm, all of which was followed by an inter-services display, fireworks and a massive bonfire.

Coronation programme, seals, coins, decoartions and giant figures of Elizabeth 1 and Sir Francis Drake.

The 'Royal' procession through Lipson Vale, with page boy Mervyn Pollard and a coach designed and made by his older brother, Terry.

There was another major bonfire in Devonport Park and all around the city the people of Plymouth celebrated, with street parties, garden parties and the crowning of community coronation queens.

Later that week there were more events in the Hoe Marquee, with the Plymouth Choral Society performing Merrie England with Frederick Harvey, Eric Greene and Ceinwen Rowlands.

Then, on Saturday 6 June, the Civic celebrations concluded at the Stadium site in Central Park with the Royal Marine Band, followed by Massed Community Singing led by the Plymouth Clarion Choir and the Reydon Singers with Dudley Savage at his Hammond organ. At the end of which there was another grand fireworks display and bonfire.

And still there was more. The following month one of the biggest spectacles ever staged on the Hoe opened on Saturday 18 July. Running through to the following Saturday, this was the grandiose 'Pageant of Plymouth Hoe', sponsored by the Plymouth Council of Social Service in co-operation with Plymouth City Council and HM Services.

CP Brown was the Chairman of the event and the production, which centred around a dozen dramatised episodes from Plymouth's history, was written by Crispin Gill, then the assistant editor of the *Western Morning News*, and produced by a well-known figure in the local amateur dramatic world, Cyril Penrose.

Hundreds of people took part and many thousands watched and among those local theatrical companies involved were the Carmenians, the Tamaritans, the Plymstock Amateur Operatic Society, the Swarthmore Settlement, Plymouth Arts Centre, the Royal Dockyard Players, the Astor Players, the Western College Players, the Mayflower Players, and the Tothill Community Centre, as well as the Boy Scouts and a number of Service groups – RAF Mount Batten, HMS *Thunderer* and 47 Coast Regiment.

The whole proceedings served to extend the wave of patriotic fervour that had been stirred up by the Coronation.

Above: *The cast of Scene 9 from the Hoe Pageant: 1643: The Siege presented by the Tothill Community Centre with the Berketex Dramatic Society, the Staff of Brown, Wills and Nicholson, Tothill Townswomen's Guild, Mount Gould Co-operative Guild, Plymouth Battalion Boys' Brigade and the Staff of Tecalemit.*
Left: *Pageant programme cover.*
Far letft: *A Coronation street party.*

243

A polling station visit by Lucy Middleton during the 1950 General Election.

POST-WAR POLITICS

When Plymouth, along with the rest of the country, went to the polls on 5 July 1945 there were a larger number of people than usual voting for the first time. It was after all ten years since the last General Election, the longest gap ever recorded and two years longer than that occasioned by the Great War.

As ever it was not easy to predict the mood of the nation, nor indeed the city, Churchill had been greatly admired as a leader of the National Government throughout the war, but Labour men like Clement Atlee, Herbert Morrison and Ernest Bevin had impressed many during those difficult times and people were prepared to believe that they could deliver on their promise of full employment, a tax-funded National Health Service and a whole-life welfare state. 'Let us face the future' was the Socialist rally cry and one that Churchill dismissed on the grounds that it would need to 'fall back on some kind of Gestapo' like body to implement such a socialist manifesto.

In the event it was Churchill that was dismissed, as a Labour landslide saw the party secure almost 50 per cent of the national vote and almost 200 seats more than the Tories, giving them an eventual overall majority of 145 seats as the Liberal vote also crumbled.

Part of the problem for the Conservatives was that there was a perception that they had lost the peace - the period between the wars that had been marked by inflation, unemployment and an initial unwillingness to re-arm in the face of a muscle-flexing Germany.

Labour party candidates and workers with Lucy Middleton and Michael Foot

Traditionally Plymouth's maritime location and its harbouring of a major naval base has been a significant ingredient in determining the political balance of the city and has at times tended to favour the Conservatives, on the grounds that *'they would best protect the nation's defence industry, which has meant that the Labour party has been less successful in Plymouth than an examination of the city's socio-economic structure would lead one to expect,'* (Rallings and Thrasher, 1991) creating a *'working-class town with middle-class politics.'* (Maguire, Brayshay and Chalkley, 1987)

Thus it was in 1918 that all three local constituencies returned Conservatives. However, in 1945, with concerns over the future of the Dockyard again and with housing a major issue, all three seats went to Labour candidates as Dockyard Engineers' Union Leader, former Lord Mayor, and local Labour Party leader, Bert Medland ousted Col. the Hon CHC Guest in Drake; Michael Foot, youngest son of the then current Lord Mayor Isaac Foot (himself a former Liberal MP for Bodmin, who had fought against Nancy Astor in 1919) defeated the former Minister of Transport, Leslie Hore Belisha in Devonport and Lucy Middleton took Nancy Astor's seat (incidentally maintaining Plymouth's female representation in Parliament and thwarting the third successive Astor, Jakey, to contest the seat).

It was the first time in Plymouth's history that neither a Conservative nor a Liberal had been returned.

Above: Michael Foot attends a community fete.

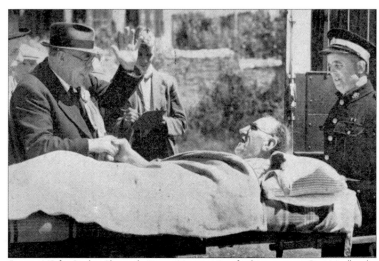

Former MP for Drake, Plymouth, Jimmy Moses voting for his successor Bert Medland.

Nancy Astor herself was encouraged not to stand, and indeed didn't. Meanwhile, her husband, Waldorf, who had been a first-class leader of the a-political council during the war, had already stood down after five years as Mayor in 1944. He *'would have accepted an alderman's seat without party attachment'*, however *'the Conservatives would have none of this; they wanted every vote, and so Lord Astor went.'* (Gill)

In 1950 the reduction of Plymouth's representation in Parliament from three seats to two meant that Bert Medland who had been *'invaluable as Plymouth's man in Westminster, fighting the reconstruction battles and making friends with vital ministers and civil servants'* (Gill) found himself without a seat as wards from Drake were transferred to both Sutton and Devonport. In the subsequent election Michael Foot and Mrs Middleton (born Lucy Cox she had married the General Secretary of the Labour Party in 1936) both held their seats with reduced majorities.

Nationally the picture was similar and although Labour were returned to power it was now with a slim majority. Following frank discussions with the King, who was concerned about going off on a tour of the Commonwealth and leaving Britain in the hands of a government that was not in the strongest of positions, Prime Minister Atlee decided to call a fresh election. Thus it was, on 25 October 1951, less than eighteen months after the previous election, with Labour hoping for a boost in their vote, the country was asked to go to the polls again.

In some respects the Socialists were successful, as, nationally, Labour secured a bigger vote than they had in 1950, and polled more votes overall than the Conservatives. But they didn't win the election, as, for only the second time in British history (the first being in 1929), the party that didn't win the popular vote won the most seats and Winston Churchill was back in No.10 Downing Street just a few weeks short of his seventy-seventh birthday.

In Plymouth the swing to the Tories helped Jakey Astor to take Lucy Middleton's Sutton seat, although the charismatic orator and huge Argyle fan, Michael Foot, was to hold on to Devonport for another four years.

The local elections too very much reflected the national picture as in 1945 the Labour party also won control of the City Council for the first time. Harry Mason, who had succeeded Lord Astor as Lord Mayor in 1944 became the first Labour leader of the Council, with Harry Wright alongside him as Chairman of Finance.

Top: *Winston Churchill in Devonport with his son, Randolph, daughter-in-law and Sir Clifford Tozer.*
Bottom: *Minister of Health, Aneurin Bevan, addressing an election meeting in Devonport.*

247

Lord Mayor Herbert Perry opens an extension to Dent's Glove Factory in the late-1940s; among those in shot, left to right; Linda Durham, Doreen Bunt, Lucy Percy, Jean Horne, Barbara Rice, Diane Rowe, Barbara Stapleton, Edna Furze (just behind the Mayor's shoulder), Barbara Jones, Kathleen Bevan, Grace Penwell, Joy Pierce, Vera Thomas, Doreen Price.

Other key posts were held by eminent Labour figures: Alderman Bill Miller (Housing), Councillor Neil Bradley (Education) and Alderman Louis Hodge (Transport).

Clifford Tozer led the Conservative opposition and "had as good a grip on his party as Mason and their bipartisan policy meant few divisions in the council.

"Mason was a modest man who would have been happier left as the chairman of the Museums and Libraries Committee, and the gentlemanly Tozer was no quick thinker," observed Crispin Gill, who as assistant editor of the Western Morning News, knew both men well. He added: *"Though party control of the council changed regularly over these years, there was basic harmony."*

The main goal was to get the City back on its feet again, and there can be no denying that those at the top had Plymouth's best interests at heart. What is more their success in acquiring the licences and the materials to address the housing situation and then the rebuilding of the City Centre, was second to none.

As another newspaper man who, as War Correspondent for the Western Morning News and Evening Herald, put it early in that post-war period: *"Many of us may not see it, but let us hope that the verdict of posterity to all who took part in the reconstruction will be - 'You have left us a great and worthy heritage'* (Pat Twyford, It Came To Our Door 1949)."

1950 Princess Alice, Countess of Athlone, received at North Road Station by Lord Mayor and Lady Mayoress, Alderman and Mrs Frank Leatherby with Deputy Chief Constable Hingston on the right. Right: Plymouth's first female Lord Mayor, Alderman Mrs Jacquetta Marshall.

249

Plymouth's Lord Mayors of the Forties and Fifties

George and Ethel Wingett, Lord Mayor and Lady Mayoress of Plymouth, 1958-9.

1939-44	Rt Hon The Viscount Astor
1944-45	Henry George Mason
1945-46	Rt Hon Isaac Foot
1946-47	W Harry Taylor
1947-49	Herbert Perry
1949-50	Frank Leatherby
1950-51	Mrs Jacquetta Marshall
1951-52	Randolph H Baker
1952-53	Henry E Wright
1953-54	Sir James Clifford Tozer
1954-55	Edmund Perry
1955-56	Edwin Broad
1956-57	William James Oats
1957-58	Leslie Francis Paul
1958-59	George John Wingett
1959-60	P N Washbourn

Top left: *Plymouth's Lord Mayor Isaac Foot pays tribute to Robert Falcon Scott, at the Scott Memorial, Mount Wise, c1946.* Top right: *Mrs Jacquetta Marshall, Lord Mayor of Plymouth 1950-51, showing the City Mace to Otowo of Owo.* Bottom left: *Lord Mayor, Randolph Baker, inspects model of a water development scheme.* Bottom right: *Lord Mayor, Alderman Harry Wright, at the Tamerton Foliot annual fruit feast, tempting young guests with strawberries.*

ACKNOWLEDGEMENTS

Many of the images that appear in this book have been supplied by readers of my Looking Back column in the Herald. In some instances they were photographs that had originally been taken for the paper back in the Forties and Fifties, but in others they are simply happy snaps that have captured the essence of the era. These wonderfully evocative shots were, more often than not, unplanned and unposed, and yet they have a magical quality which adds much to this review.

The archives of the Herald and Western Morning News have also been immensely useful - thanks go to Alan Qualtrough, Bill Martin, and Pete Holgate. The bulk of this material is now curated by the Plymouth Barbican Asssociation's South West Image Bank on the Barbican - thanks there go to the Directors and their archivist Stacey Dyer.

The Plymouth Central Library Local Studies Department (notably the Broderick Collection) and the Plymouth City Museum and Art Gallery (Goodrich Collection) have also been very helpful.

Another significant source of images has been that well-loved, erstwhile must-have, local yearbook 'Doidges Annual', a valuable source of stories and photographs that sadly stopped in 1955.

Dingles and the Plymouth Co-operative Society have been a valuable source of material. So too have old books, tourist guides, brochures, and souvenir programmes have also proved useful, as did the inevitable collections of old picture postcards.

From a practical and personal perspective, I'd also like to express very grateful thanks to my publisher Clare (who is also my best friend and long-suffering wife), sister-in-law Helen, mother-in-law Patricia and Bill Bugler, all of whom have read this looking for typos and other irritants, as indeed have my equally long-suffering Barbican team, Rob Warren and Doreen Mole, who keep the shop on the road and all my Looking Back bits and pieces in order.

Main photo: *Budding local photographer Roy Westlake in 1948.* Left: *Roy's first published photograph - summer of '49. His mother, his niece and his Austin 7 looking across to Sheepstor Village. Over the next few decades Roy would take hundreds of photographs for local travel – and tourist – guides and books.*

Right: The author with his grandfather, Stewart Robinson, in April 1955, together with a selection of his grandparents ration books issued while they were living in Tothill Road, St Judes in the late-forties, early-fifties.

Meanwhile, the A-Z list of those individuals who have sent me photographs over the last ten years or so - photographs that have helped make this book what it is - is the longest of any book I've produced so far, I only hope I haven't left anyone out!

So thank you: Gary and Lisa Andrews, Francis Baker, Phil Barrow, Victor Barton, Ian Bickle, Guy Belshaw, Tony Benwell, Robin Blythe-Lord, Margaret Bond, John and Sylvia Boulden, Geoff Bowden, Tom Bowden, Graham and Pat Brooks, Jean Brown, Paul Burtnyk, Dessie Carnell, Tim Charlesworth, Jean Chapman, Mina Chapman, Arthur Clamp, Fred Colton, Roger Compton, Bob Cook, Sheila Cook, Toni Cook, Harvey Crane, Bernice Dann, Maurice Dart, Sue Down, Brian Elliott, Andy Endacott, Marilyn Endacott, Dennis Escott, Guy Fleming, Dougie Flood, Arthur Folland, Michael Foot, Edna Furze, Brian Gadd, Crispin Gill, Duncan Godefroy, Jean Gray, Tom Greaves, Micahel Greenwood, Jim Griffin, Terry Guswell, Barbara Hampshire, Audrey Harrison, John Harvey, Gary Hayes, Barry Henderson, Ron Hellyer, Ken Hill, Norman Hine, Derek Hiscock, Graham Hobbins, Tom Hobbs, Linda Hoblyn, Mike Hocking, Robin Hoskins, Daryl Jago, David Jennings, Doreen Johnson, Sue Johns, Gillian Kent, David King, Alan Kittridge, Ivan Lang, Ray McSweeny, Ann Maddern, Peter Moate, Brian Moseley, Jimmy Moses, John Mulinder, Eileen Normington, Jean Norsworthy, Sid Oliver, Babs Owen, Ann Pallant, Mike Parriss, May Parson, Mike Pearse, Joe Pengelly, Jean Perkins, Sandy Pimlott, John Pinch, Frank Pocock, Merv Pollard, Bob Pratt, Keith Pring, Denise Putt, Des Robinson, Liz Rook, Janet Scoles, Charlie Sells, Dave Sharp. Gordon Sparks, Jeanette Simpson, Reg Smith, Len Stevens, Joan Stopperton, Bill Strauss, Derek Tait, Peter Taylor, Art Thomas, Alan Tibbitts, Roy Todd, Sid Tonkin, David Tozer, Don Tucker, Mike Turpitt, Peter and Joy Vittle, Shirley Walker, John Walters, Jimmy Warren, Rob Warren, Peter Warrren, Gerald Wasley, Peter Waterhouse, Roy Westlake, Mike White, Mary Wills, Jonathan Wood, Teddy Woodhouse and Sonia Wright.

Chris Robinson *October 2011*

BIBLIOGRAPHY

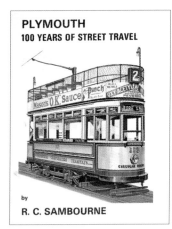

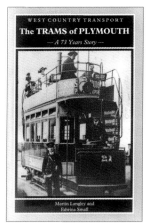

A Century of Plymouth: Events, People and Places over the last 100 years – **Guy Fleming**, Sutton Publishing Ltd (2000)

Achievement 1946-49 – Plymouth Labour Party (1949)

All About Argyle 1903-1963 – **WS Tonkin**, Diamond Jubilee Book (1963)

Anderton and Rowland's Illusion & Reality – **Kevin Scrivens & Stephen Smith**, Fairground Heritage Trust (2008)

Chronicle of the Royal Western Yacht Club of England 1900-1977 – **Capt. TWB Shaw**, Suttons (1984)

Devon at the Cinema: An Illustrated History of Cinema Going – **Gordon Chapman**, Devon Books (2000)

Devonport Dockyard Railway – **Paul Burkhalter**, Twelveheads Press (1996)

Devonport Dockyard Story – **Lt Cdr Ken Burns**, Maritime Books (1984)

Elizabethan Plymouth – **Chris Robinson**, Pen & Ink (2002)

Doidge's Western Counties Illustrated Annual – (1940-1954 inclusive)

Electricity in Plymouth: Its Origins and Development – **Edward W Luscombe**, The Devonshire Association (1999)

Family Britain 1951-57 – **David Kynaston**, Bloomsbury (2009)

The Fifties – **Peter Lewis**, Heinemann (1978)

Fleet History of Plymouth Corporation and Plymouth Citybus Limited – The P.S.V

From Rattles to Radio, A History of Plymouth City Police Force, **Ernest Dickaty**, type-script (1977)

Golden Age of Radio – **Denis Gifford**, Batsford (1985)

The Historic Defences of Plymouth – **Andrew Pye & Freddie Woodward**, Cornwall County Council (1996)

A History of Devon County Football Association 1888 - 1988 – **Sam Rendell** (1988)

A History of Devonport – **Chris Robinson**, Pen & Ink (2010)

A History of Plymouth: And Her Neighbours – **C.W. Bracken**, Underhill (Plymouth) Ltd (1931)

Images of Plymouth – **Tom Bowden**, Sutton Publishing (2006)

Images of England: Plymouth – **Derek Tait**, Tempus Publishing Ltd (2003)

Introduction To Plymouth and Neighbourhood – Plymouth Corporation of Tramways & Transport Department Offices, Bowering Press (1926)

Isaac Foot: A Westcountry Boy – Apostle of England – **Michael Foot and Alison Highet**, Politico's Publishing Ltd (2006)

It Came To Our Door – **H.P. Twyford revised by Chris Robinson**, Pen & Ink Publishing (2005)

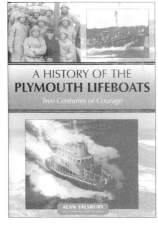    

Kelly's Post Office Directory of Plymouth and District – (1940, 1951, 1953))
The Making of the University of Plymouth – **Alston Kennerley**, University of Plymouth
Nancy, Lady Astor Sunshine of Plymouth – **Vicky Norman**, Joseph Louei (2009)
Naval Heritage in The West: Part I, II & III – **Andy Endacott** (1986, 1987, 1988)
Newton Abbot to Plymouth – **Vic Mitchell & Keith Smith**, Middleton Press (2001)
North Prospect/ Swilly/ North Prospect – **Kenneth D. Tapscott** (2008)
150 Years of the Co-operative in Plymouth – **Chris Robinson**, Pen & Ink (2009)
Oval Racing in Devon and Cornwall – **Andrew Weltch**, Tempus (2003)
Playbill: A History of Theatre in the Westcountry – **Harvey Crane**, Macdonald and Evans Ltd (1980)
Plymouth: A New History – **Crispin Gill**, Devon Books (1993)
Plymouth: As Time Draws On Vols 1 & 2 – **Chris Robinson**, Pen & Ink Publishing (1985, 1988)
Plymouth Bygones: Sixty Years of Memories and Pictures – **Guy Fleming**, Devon Books (1991)
Plymouth Civil Service Sports & Leisure Club, 75th Anniversary – Mirror Image (2002)
Plymouth College, The First Hundred Years – **Chris Robinson**, Pen & Ink Publishing (2005)
Plymouth Cricket Club 1857-2007 – **Phil Barrow**, Plymouth CC (2007)
Plymouth in Pictures – **Crispin Gill**, W J Holman Ltd (1968)
Plymouth in War & Peace – **Guy Fleming**, Bossiney Books (1987)
Plymouth: Maritime City in Transition – **Brian Chalkley, David Dunkerley, Peter Gripaios**, David & Charles (1991)
Plymouth: More Pictures from the Past – **Guy Fleming**, The Devonshire Press Ltd (1996)
Plymouth: Official Guide – The Entertainments and Publicity Department of the City Council, Underhill Ltd (1939, 1940))
Plymouth: Ocean Liner, Port of Call – **Alan Kittridge**, Twelveheads Press (1993)
Plymouth: Pictures from the Past – **Guy Fleming**, The Devonshire Press Ltd (1995)
Plymouth River: A History of the Laira and Cattewater – **Crispin Gill**, Devon Books (1997)
Plymouth Speedway – **Paul Eustace**, Tempus Publishing Ltd (2006)
Plymouth to St. Austell – **Vic Mitchell & Keith Smith**, Middleton Press (2001)

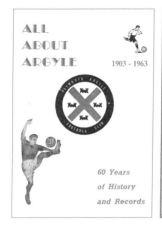   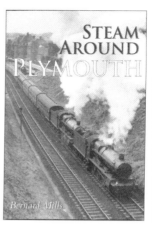 

Plymouth Vision of a Modern City – **Jeremy Gould,** English Heritage (2010)

Plymouth Yesterday Today – **Vic Saundercock** (1989)

Plymouth 100 Years of Street Travel – **R.C. Sambourne,** Glasney Press (circa 1970)

Plymouth 1848 - 1958 – **Crispin Gill,** Plymouth Y.M.C.A. (1958)

Plymouth's Golden Age of Trams – **Arthur L. Clamp,** P.D.S. Printers Ltd (circa 1985)

Plymouth's Historic Barbican – **Chris Robinson,** Pen & Ink Publishing (2007)

The Radio Companion – **Paul Donovan,** Grafton (1991)

Royal Visits to Devon and Cornwall: Images from the WMN and Evening Herald 1900 - 2000 – **John Van Der Kiste,** Halsgrove (2002)

Scouting in Plymouth 1908 - 1982 – **Graham E. Brooks and Arthur L. Clamp,** P.D.S. Printers Ltd (1982)

The Second Book of Plymouth - **W. Best Harris,** Oakfield Press (circa 1960)

Ships in Plymouth Sound – **Sydney Goodman,** Halsgrove (1999)

Showmen of the Past: Hancocks of the West – **Kevin Scrivens & Stephen Smith,** New Era Publications (2006)

Speedway in the South-West – **Tony Lethbridge,** Tempus Publishing Inc (2003)

A Sporting Century 1863 - 1963 – **Anne Pallant,** Anne Pallant (1997)

Steam Around Plymouth – **Bernard Mills,** Tempus Publishing Ltd (2003)

The Story of Langdon Court – **Robin Blythe-Lord** (2008)

The Story of Plymouth – **R.A.J Walling,** London Westaway Books (1950)

Sutton Harbour – **Crispin Gill,** Devon Books (1997)

Tamaritans Theatre Company A History 1931-2007 - **Chris Hunt,** Hunt (2008)

300 Years Devotion to Duty – **Andy Endacott** (1991)

The Trams of Plymouth: A 73 - Year Story – **Martin Langley and Edwina Small,** Ex Libris Press (1990)

Union Street – **Chris Robinson,** Pen & Ink (2000)

Victorian Plymouth: As Time Draws On – **Chris Robinson,** Pen & Ink Publishing (1991)

The Wartime House: Home life in Wartime Britain 1939 - 1945 – **Mike Brown & Carol Harris,** Sutton Publishing Ltd (2005)

T. Whitelegg and Sons': Cavalcade of Shows – **Guy Belshaw,** New Era publications (2005)